EP Zoology
Printables:
Levels 5-8

This book belongs to:

_____

This book was made for your convenience. It is available for printing from the Easy Peasy All-in-One Homeschool website. It contains all of the printables from Easy Peasy's zoology course. The instructions for each page are found in the online course.

Easy Peasy All-in-One Homeschool is a free online homeschool curriculum providing high quality education for children around the globe. It provides complete courses for preschool through high school graduation. For EP's curriculum visit allinonehomeschool.com.

EP Zoology Printables: Levels 5-8

This workbook, made by Tina Rutherford with permission from Easy Peasy All-in-One Homeschool, is based on the zoology component of Easy Peasy's curriculum. For EP's online curriculum visit allinonehomeschool.com.

ISBN: 9798640339970

First Edition: June 2020

Mammal Classification

Cut out each hexagon and sort the mammals by category.

Monotremes
lay eggs

Marsupials
have pouches

Carnivores
eat meat

Pinnipeds
have flippers

Ungulates
have hooves

Primates
have forward-facing eyes, opposable thumbs, and big brains

(This page left intentionally blank)

Mammal Classification

Cetaceans
aquatic, have
blowholes

Sirenians
large, herbivorous,
water-dwelling

Rodents
Have large incisors
for gnawing

Insectivores
Small, eat insects
and other small
animals

platypus

lion

(This page left intentionally blank)

Mammal Classification

manatee

koala

walrus

squirrel

wombat

dolphin

(This page left intentionally blank)

Mammal Classification

lemur

kangaroo

bear

ape

cow

whale

(This page left intentionally blank)

Mammal Classification

mole

zebra

capybara

seal

badger

pig

(This page left intentionally blank)

Mammal Classification

prairie dog

camel

beaver

rhino

hedgehog

monkey

(This page left intentionally blank)

Invertebrate Classification

Cut out each hexagon and sort the invertebrates by category.

Arthropods
jointed legs and an exoskeleton

Mollusks
soft-bodied, sometimes have shells

Worms
long cylindrical tube-like body, no limbs, and no eyes

Echinoderms
spiny-skinned, suction-tubed "feet"

Poriferans
sponges

Cnidarians
hollow-bodied, tentacles, stinging cells

(This page left intentionally blank)

Invertebrate Classification

earthworm

spongia

scorpion

jellyfish

octopus

starfish

(This page left intentionally blank)

Invertebrate Classification

centipede

sea anemone

sea urchin

lobster

grasshopper

snail

(This page left intentionally blank)

Invertebrate Classification

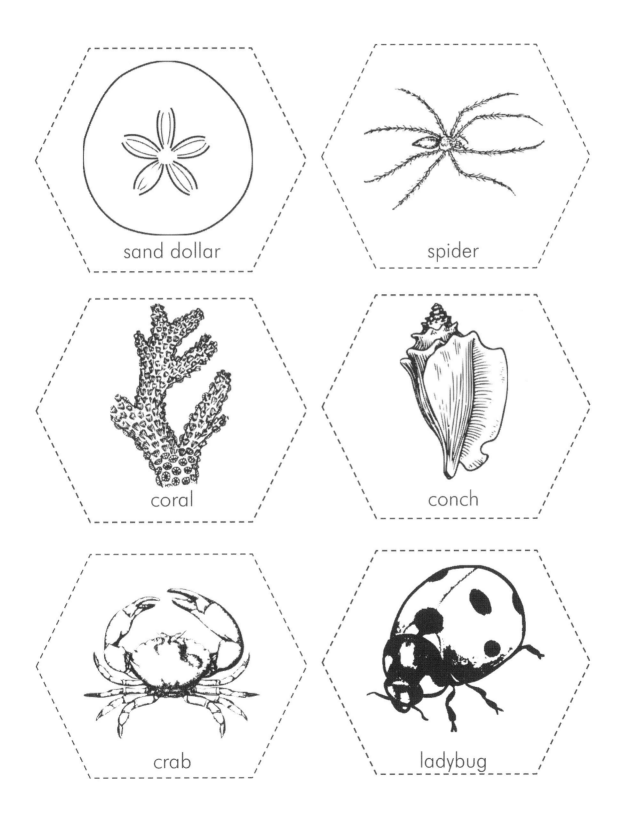

sand dollar

spider

coral

conch

crab

ladybug

(This page left intentionally blank)

What Did You Learn?

Fill in the blank with the word that best fits.

mammals	arthropods	fish	reptiles	vertebrates
invertebrates	sponges	birds	mollusks	

have a backbone   _____

have hair; give birth to live young   _____

air-breathing; covered with scales   _____

largest group of animals   _____

don't have a backbone   _____

have feathers; lay eggs   _____

soft-bodied or shelled   _____

pores throughout their bodies   _____

live in the water all their lives   _____

(This page left intentionally blank)

Endangered Species

Cut the pages on the dotted lines and place them in this pattern: $\begin{smallmatrix}1 & 2\\3 & 4\end{smallmatrix}$ Using a single six-sided die and whatever markers you can gather (coins, different rocks, pawns from other games, etc.), take turns rolling and moving the number on the die. Follow the directions on the square you land on. Requested facts can be found throughout the board. Can you all get to the end before you go extinct?

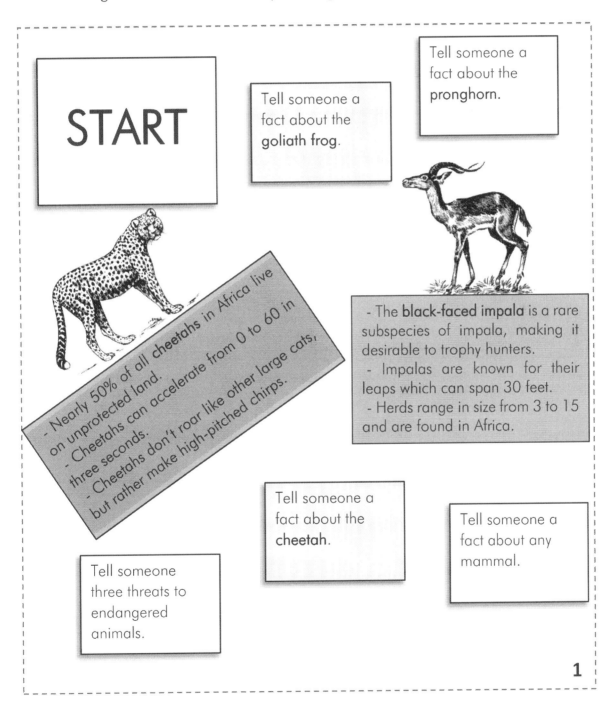

START

Tell someone a fact about the **goliath frog**.

Tell someone a fact about the **pronghorn.**

- Nearly 50% of all cheetahs in Africa live on unprotected land.
- Cheetahs can accelerate from 0 to 60 in three seconds.
- Cheetahs don't roar like other large cats, but rather make high-pitched chirps.

- The **black-faced impala** is a rare subspecies of impala, making it desirable to trophy hunters.
- Impalas are known for their leaps which can span 30 feet.
- Herds range in size from 3 to 15 and are found in Africa.

Tell someone a fact about the **cheetah**.

Tell someone a fact about any mammal.

Tell someone three threats to endangered animals.

1

(This page left intentionally blank)

Tell someone a fact about an African animal.

Tell someone a fact about the **impala**.

Your species moves from the **threatened** list to the **endangered** list. Lose a turn!

Tell someone a fact about a non-mammal.

- The **Sonoran pronghorn** is one of the most endangered animals in the United States.
- The pronghorn is the fastest land animal in North America.
- Drought is its biggest threat.

Tell someone three threats to endangered animals.

Tell someone a fact about the **blue whale**.

Tell someone a fact about the **cockatoo**.

Move forward three spaces and read that square.

Catch a poacher in the act and save an elephant. Roll again!

2

(This page left intentionally blank)

3

Tell someone a fact about the **goliath frog**.

Tell someone a fact about a non-mammal.

Tell someone a fact about the **impala**.

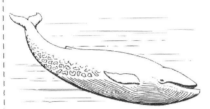

- The **blue whale** is the largest animal known to have existed.
- Whaling (hunting whales for their usable products) is its biggest threat.
- Seen regularly off the coast of California.

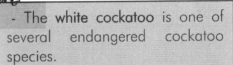

- The **white cockatoo** is one of several endangered cockatoo species.
- Its beauty makes it desirable for the pet trade
- Found in the Philippines, Indonesia, and Australia.

FINISH

Recite three things you've learned and your species will survive!

Tell any fact that hasn't been told so far to avoid extinction!

Tell someone three threats to endangered animals.

(This page left intentionally blank)

4

Tell someone a fact about the **blue whale**.

Tell someone a fact about an African animal.

Tell someone a fact about the **cockatoo**.

Discover a new population of an endangered species: roll again!

- The **goliath frog** is the largest living frog on earth.
- It is found in a few remote places such as Equatorial Guinea.
- Its biggest threat is its desirability as an exotic pet.

Tell someone a fact about the **cheetah**.

Tell someone a fact about a mammal.

Tell someone a fact about a non-African animal.

Make it to the finish space on your next turn or become EXTINCT.

Tell someone a fact about the **pronghorn**.

(This page left intentionally blank)

Food Chain

Fill in this worksheet with examples.

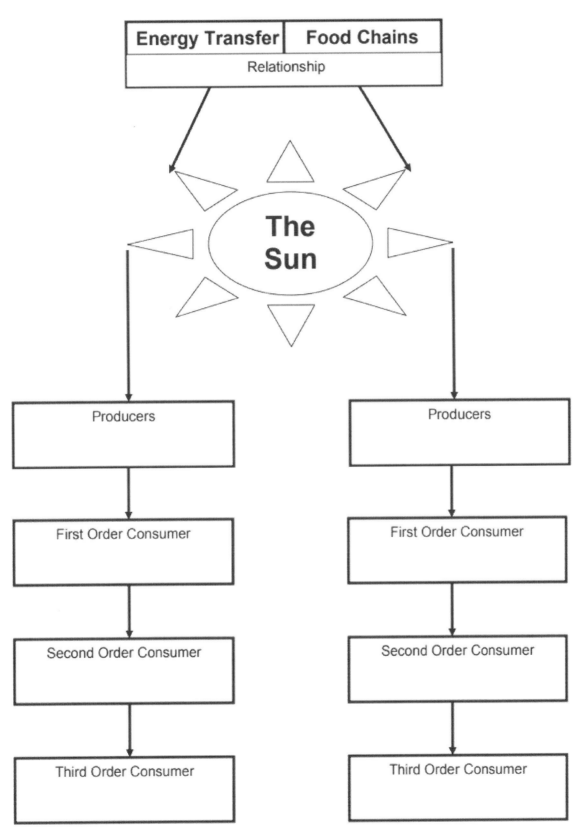

Energy Transfer	Food Chains
Relationship	

The Sun

Producers		Producers

First Order Consumer		First Order Consumer

Second Order Consumer		Second Order Consumer

Third Order Consumer		Third Order Consumer

(This page left intentionally blank)

Hibernation

Migration

Adaptation

(This page left intentionally blank)

Wake or Sleep

Cut out the rectangle as one piece and fold on the center line. Cut on the dotted line to the center fold. Inside (opposite the "glue here" side), glue each animal under the appropriate flap based on whether it wakes to eat or sleeps all winter.

brown bat	ladybug	gopher	turtle	squirrel
chipmunk	snake	frog	bear	skunk

(This page left intentionally blank)

Hibernation

Cut out each piece as one and fold them in half. Answer the question about hibernation inside that piece. In the squirrel piece, write how animals prepare for winter by continuously eating.

(glue here)

What is hibernation?

(This page left intentionally blank)

Hibernation

Cut out the rectangle as one piece. Fold the left side in (on the line at A), and fold the right side in (on the line at B). Cut on the dotted line so that there are two strips you can open to the fold. On the inside (opposite "glue here"), write about the changes in breathing and body temperature an animal in hibernation experiences.

Breathing

Body Temperature

↑ A

(glue here)

↓ B

What bodily changes occur during hibernation?

Turtles and Snakes

Cut out the rectangle as one piece and fold on the center line. Cut on the dotted line. Write the answer inside on the backside of the flaps. On the inside (opposite the "glue here" side), write WHY turtles and snakes sleep for the winter where they do. Use complete sentences.

(glue here)

Where do they sleep?

Turtles   Snakes

(This page left intentionally blank)

Migration

Cut out the rectangles and fold on the dotted line. Inside (opposite the "glue here" side), answer the questions in complete sentences.

(glue here)

What is migration?

(glue here)

Why do some birds fly south for the winter?

(This page left intentionally blank)

Migration

Cut out the rectangle as one piece and fold on the center line. On the inside (opposite the "glue here" side), answer the question. On the next page, draw the migration routes for the birds listed. Be sure to color in the key with the colors you use for each bird's route.

(glue here)

Which birds fly south for the winter?

(This page left intentionally blank)

Migration Routes

Atlantic Flyway ☐

Mississippi Flyway ☐

Central Flyway ☐

Pacific Flyway ☐

N →

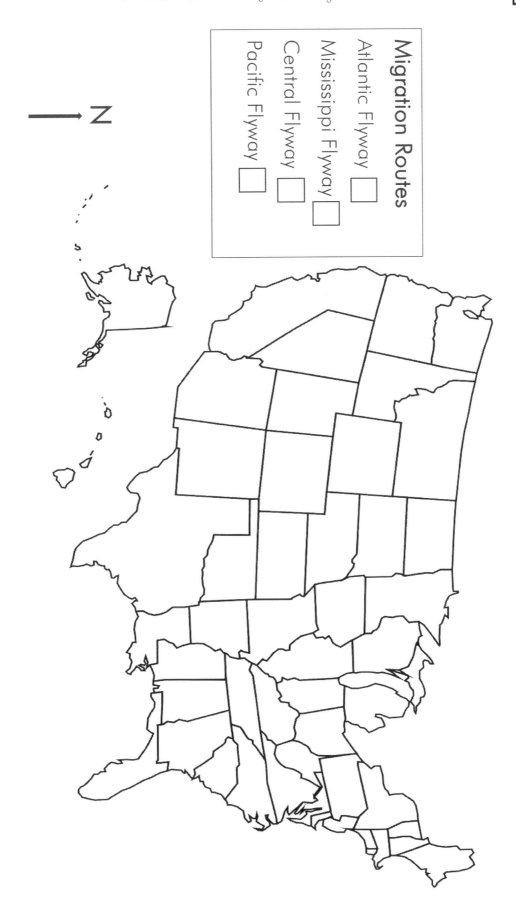

(This page left intentionally blank)

Adaptation

Cut out the hexagons and fold on the middle line. Inside (opposite the "glue here" side), answer the questions in complete sentences.

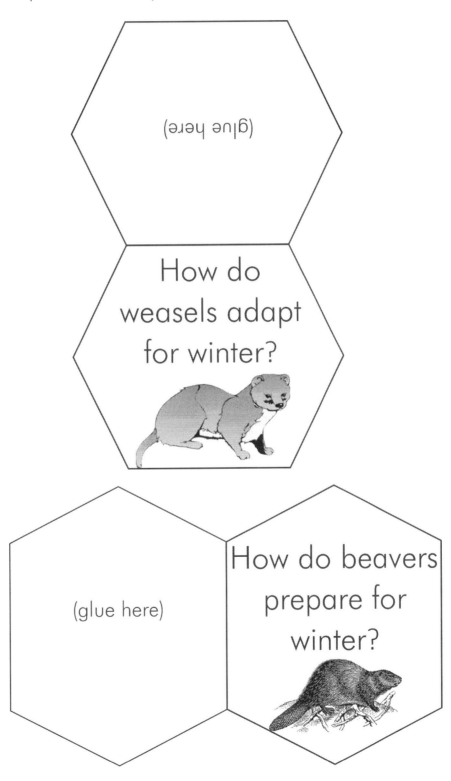

(glue here)

How do weasels adapt for winter?

(glue here)

How do beavers prepare for winter?

(This page left intentionally blank)

Adaptation

Cut out the hexagons and fold on the middle line. Inside (opposite the "glue here" side), answer the questions in complete sentences.

(glue here)

How do foxes adapt to winter weather?

(glue here)

What does it mean to adapt?

(This page left intentionally blank)

All
About
Lizards

(This page left intentionally blank)

Classification

Cut out the rectangle as one piece. Fold the left side in (on the line at A), and fold the right side in (on the line at B). Cut on the dotted lines so that Kingdom, Phylum, Class, and Order are strips you can open to the fold. On the inside (opposite "glue here"), fill in the information.

Kingdom

Phylum

Class

Order

A →

(glue here)

B ↓

Classification
of
Lizards

(This page left intentionally blank)

Reptiles

Cut out the hexagons and fold on the middle line. Inside (opposite the "glue here" side), write the characteristics of reptiles and some examples of other reptiles.

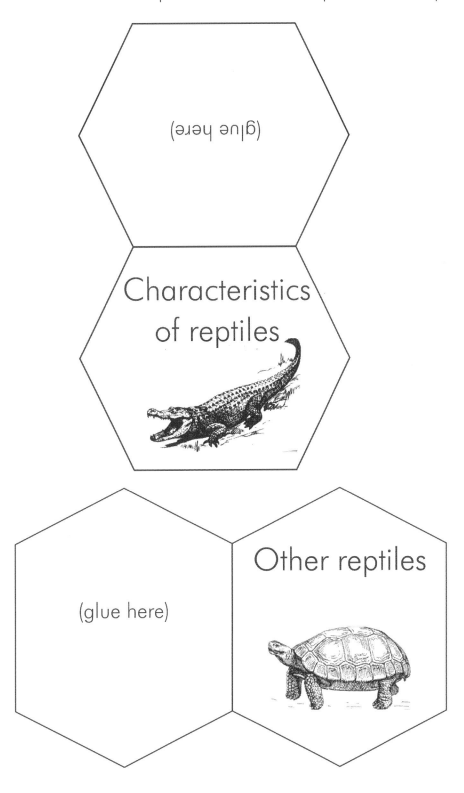

(glue here)

Characteristics
of reptiles

(glue here)

Other reptiles

(This page left intentionally blank)

Vocabulary

Cut out the rocks and write the definitions to the vocabulary words they contain.
Use the lizard as the cover piece and staple on the side.

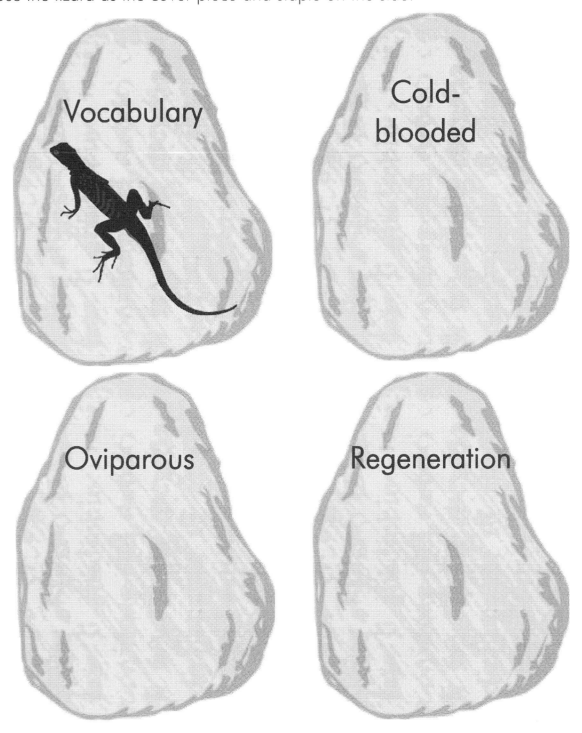

Vocabulary

Cold-blooded

Oviparous

Regeneration

(This page left intentionally blank)

Location

Color in the locations on the world map where lizards are found. You can make a key and color different colors for different types of lizards if you want to do further research. Cut the big rectangle as one piece and fold the outside squares to cover the world map. Glue the label pieces on top of the folded piece.

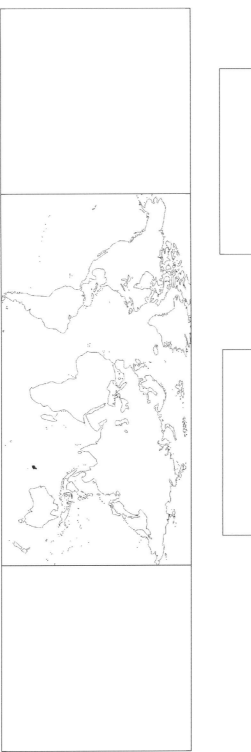

Lizard

Locations

(This page left intentionally blank)

Predators

Cut out the rectangle as one piece and fold on the dotted line. Inside (opposite the "glue here" side), write some of the predators of lizards. You can also draw pictures if you'd like.

(glue here)

Predators of lizards

Zoology
Levels 5-8

(This page left intentionally blank)

Defense

Cut out the rectangle as one piece and fold on the dotted line. Inside (opposite the "glue here" side), write or cut and paste the different types of defense mechanisms a lizard has.

(glue here)

A lizard's defense

| camouflage | sharp spines | slippery scales |

strong, swinging tails

(This page left intentionally blank)

Lizard senses

Cut each piece out in full (don't cut off the tab label). Write information on each piece. Stack the pieces in this order top to bottom: Lizard senses, sight, smell, hearing.

Lizard senses

How do lizards see?

sight

(This page left intentionally blank)

How do lizards smell?

smell

How do lizards hear?

hearing

(This page left intentionally blank)

Lizard Food

Cut out the rectangle and fold on the dotted line. Inside (opposite the "glue here" side), write what lizards eat. You can draw pictures if you'd like.

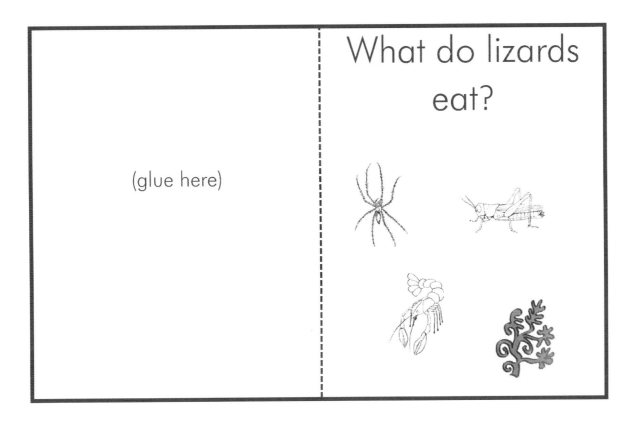

(This page left intentionally blank)

(This page left intentionally blank)

Types of Lizards

Cut each piece out in full and fold each piece on the dotted line. Write facts about each type of lizard inside the piece, then glue the three small pieces side by side inside of the large piece.

(glue here)

Types of Lizards

(This page left intentionally blank)

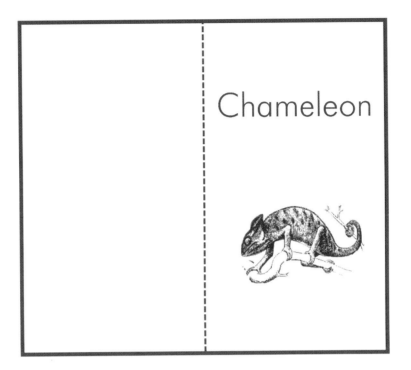

Chameleon

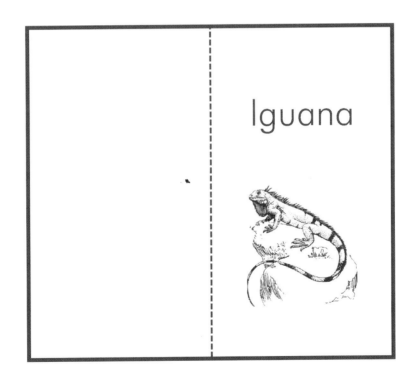

Iguana

(This page left intentionally blank)

Gila
monster

(This page left intentionally blank)

Lizard facts

Cut out the hexagons and stack them with the "facts" piece on top. Fill in the blank pieces with any facts you've learned about lizards that you didn't get to include elsewhere in the book. Staple and add to your lapbook.

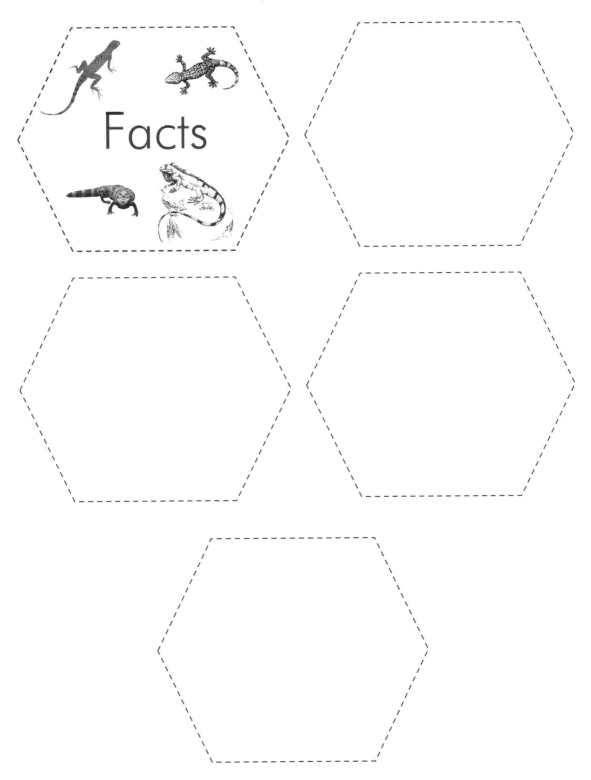

(This page left intentionally blank)

Lapbook pieces

Cut out the rectangle as one piece. Fold the left side in (on the line at **A**), and fold the right side in (on the line at **B**). Cut on the dotted lines so you have four strips you can label and open to the fold. On the inside (opposite "glue here"), write your information. On the right panel, create a title and add artwork if you'd like.

↑ A

(glue here)

B ↓

(This page left intentionally blank)

Lapbook pieces

Cut out the rectangle as one piece and fold on the center line. Cut on the dotted line to the center fold. Label the two flaps. Inside (opposite the "glue here" side), write your information.

(glue here)

(This page left intentionally blank)

Lapbook pieces

Cut out the rectangles and fold on the dotted line. Label the right side and add artwork if you'd like. Inside (opposite the "glue here" side), write your information.

(glue here)

(glue here)

(This page left intentionally blank)

(glue here)

(glue here)

(This page left intentionally blank)

Lapbook pieces

Cut out the hexagons. Add a title and/or artwork to one piece and information to the other pieces. Stack them and staple on the side to make a book.

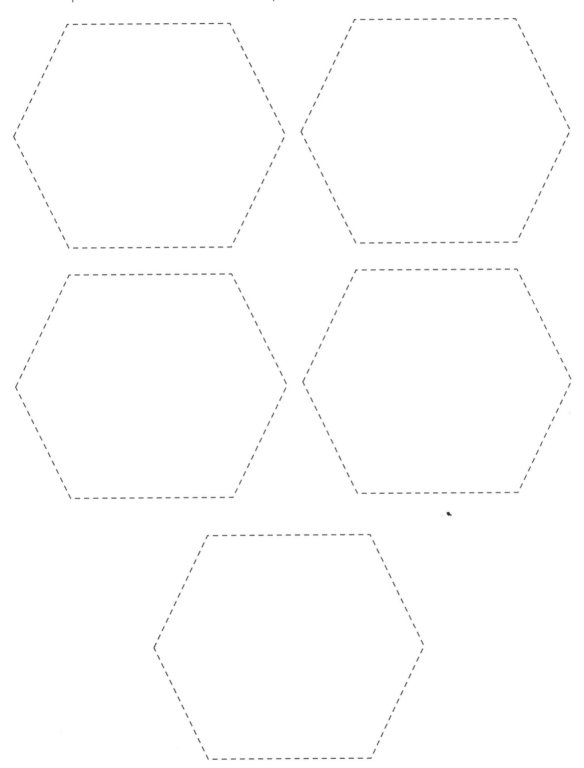

(This page left intentionally blank)

Lapbook pieces

Cut out the rectangle as one piece and fold on the dotted line. Give the piece a title and/or artwork. Inside (opposite the "glue here" side), write your information.

(glue here)

(This page left intentionally blank)

(glue here)

(This page left intentionally blank)

Lapbook pieces

Cut each piece out in full (don't cut off the tab label). The piece without the tab is the cover – add a title and/or artwork. Be sure to label each tab and stack them in order: cover, left tab, center tab, right tab.

(This page left intentionally blank)

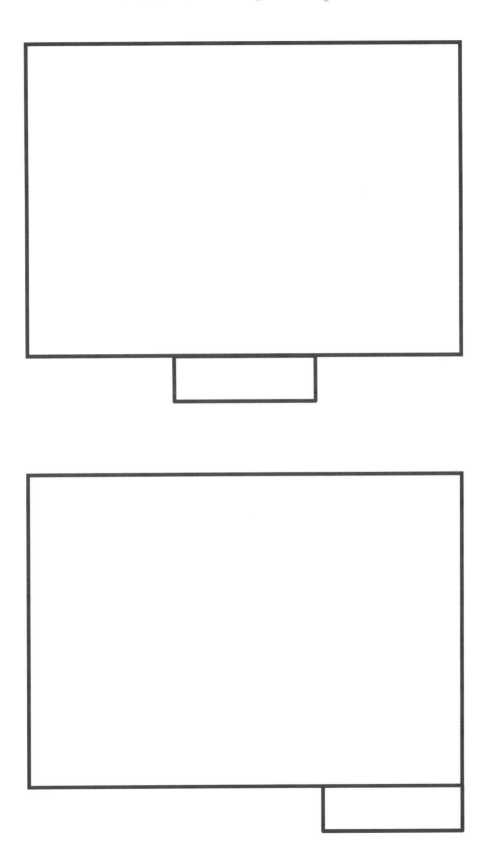

(This page left intentionally blank)

Lapbook Pieces

Cut each piece out in full and fold each piece on the dotted line. Write a title on the big book. Give each small book a topic and put facts inside. Glue the three small pieces side by side inside of the large piece.

(glue here)

(This page left intentionally blank)

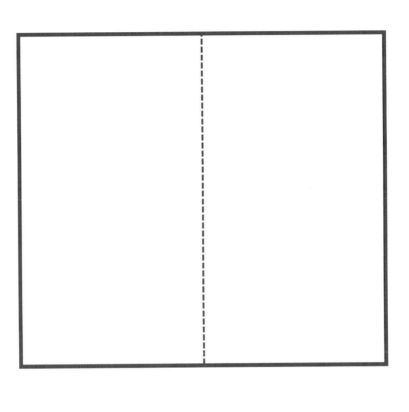

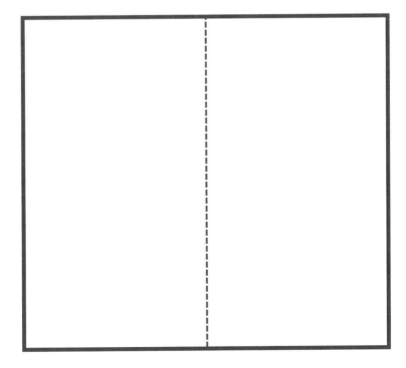

(This page left intentionally blank)

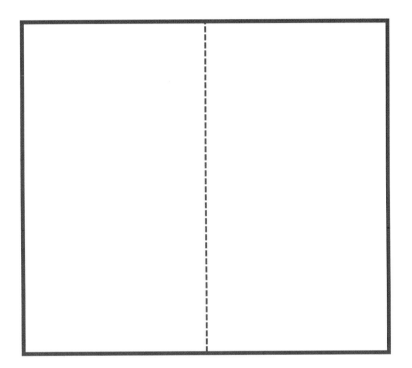

(This page left intentionally blank)

Lapbook pieces

Cut around the outside of the first circle, as well as along the dotted lines to cut out the "cut out here" section. Put a title and/or artwork on this circle. Cut around the outside of the second circle. Fill each wedge of the circle with a fact (you can add more artwork if you have too many wedges). Stack the first circle on the second circle and secure with a brad.

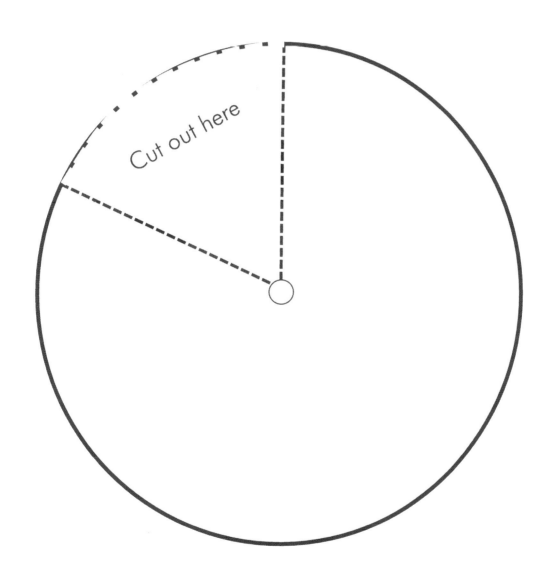

Cut out here

(This page left intentionally blank)

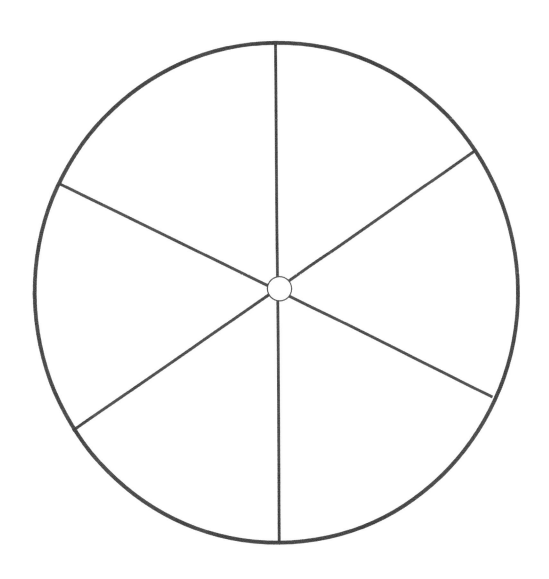

(This page left intentionally blank)

All About Eagles

(This page left intentionally blank)

Lesson
69

Eagle stats

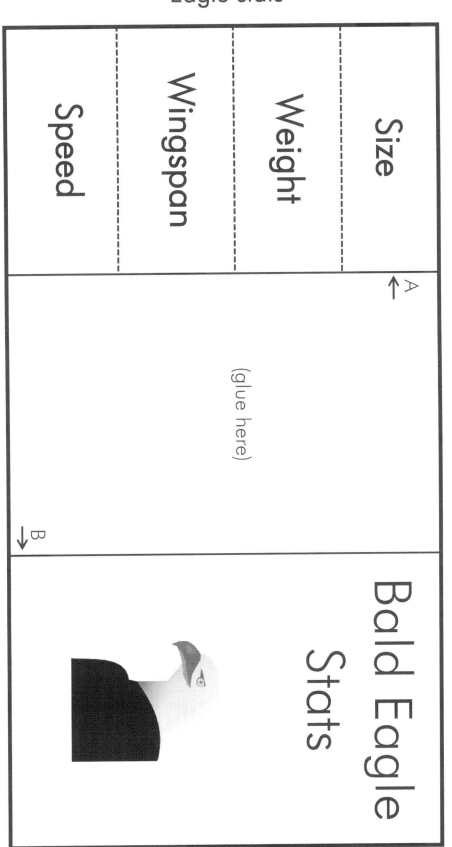

Size

Weight

Wingspan

Speed

A →

(glue here)

B ↓

Bald Eagle
Stats

Cut out the rectangle as one piece. Fold the left side in (on the line at A), and fold the right side in (on the line at B). Cut on the dotted lines so that the four categories are strips you can open to the fold. On the inside (opposite "glue here"), write the information for that category.

(This page left intentionally blank)

Where Do They Live?

Cut out the rectangles and fold on the dotted line. Inside (opposite the "glue here" side), write about bald eagle habitats and nests.

(glue here)

Habitat

(glue here)

Nests

(This page left intentionally blank)

Eagle Diet

Cut around the outside of the first circle, as well as along the dotted lines to cut out the "cut out here" section. Cut around the outside of the second circle. Stack the first circle on the second circle and secure with a brad.

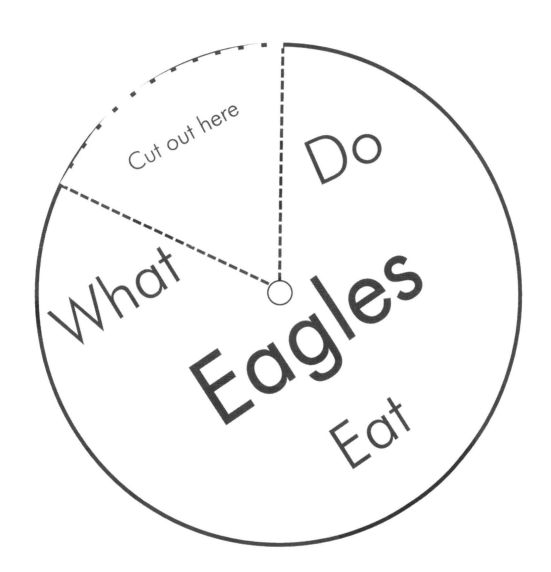

Cut out here

Do

What

Eagles

Eat

(This page left intentionally blank)

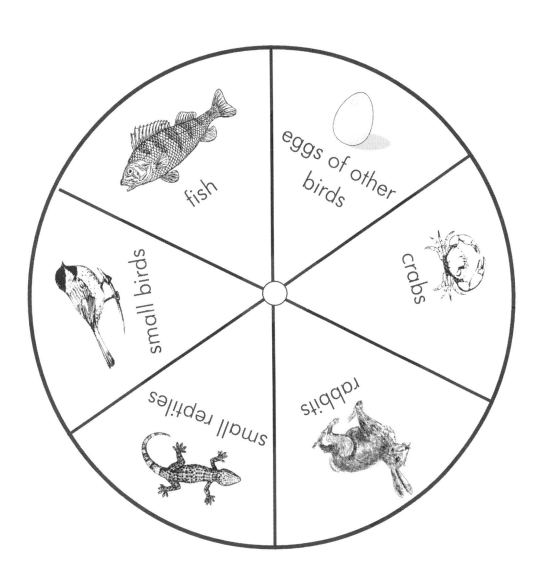

(This page left intentionally blank)

Eagles in the Nations

Cut out the rectangle as one piece and fold on the dotted line. Inside (opposite the "glue here" side), write or paste the various countries around the world that use the eagle as the national bird.

(glue here)

National Bird

(This page left intentionally blank)

(This page left intentionally blank)

Germany

Kazakhstan

Mexico

United States

Austria

(This page left intentionally blank)

Bible Verses

Cut out as one piece. Fold up bottom. Then fold back side tabs and secure to the back flap. You have made a pocket to hold the verse cards in your lapbook. Cut out the verse cards. Use the blank cards to copy down more verses if you'd like – there are lots of mentions of eagles in the Bible! Store them in the pocket.

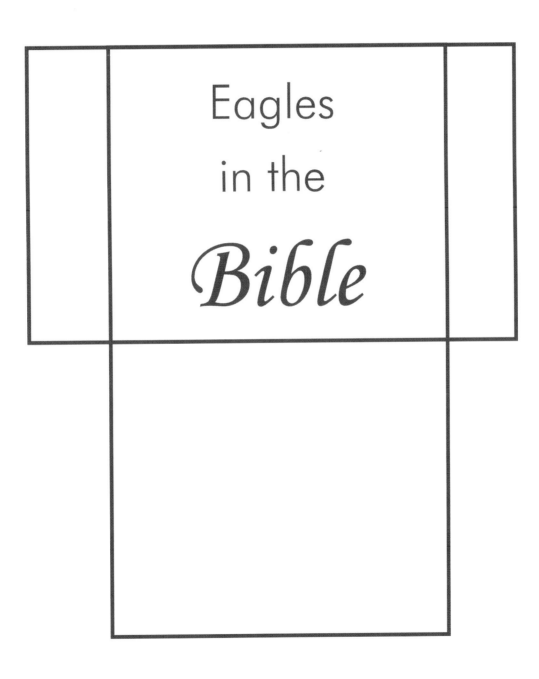

Eagles
in the
Bible

(This page left intentionally blank)

Psalm 103:5

"He fills my life with good things. My youth is renewed like the eagle's."

Exodus 19:4

"You have seen what I did to the Egyptians. You know how I carried you on eagles' wings and brought you to myself."

Isaiah 40:31

"But those who trust in the Lord will find new strength. They will soar high on wings like eagles. They will run and not grow weary. They will walk and not faint."

(This page left intentionally blank)

(This page left intentionally blank)

Location

Color in the locations on the world map where eagles are found. You can make a key and color different colors for different times of the year if you want to do further research. Cut the big rectangle as one piece and fold the outside squares to cover the world map. Glue the label pieces on top of the folded piece.

Eagle

Locations

(This page left intentionally blank)

Other Facts

Cut out the eggs and write other interesting facts you've learned about bald eagles.

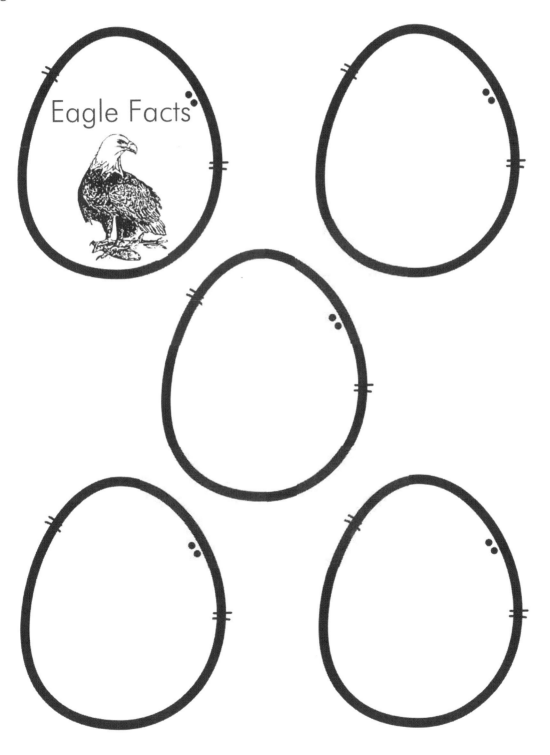

Eagle Facts

(This page left intentionally blank)

Animal Mimicry

Fill in the crossword puzzle using the reading linked online.

Across:

4. A striped _____ uses aposematic coloration.
6. Katydids mimic these
7. Appearance and _____ are both important in crypsis.
8. Fritz Müller studied this.

Down:

1. When an animal blends with its environment.
2. Bates collected edible and inedible _____.
3. Many _____ use the "lying-in-wait" technique.
5. Warning through colors is also known as _____ coloration.
9. The person or thing being mimicked

(This page left intentionally blank)

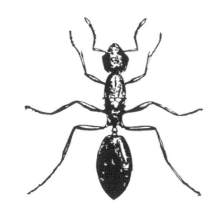

All
About
Ants

(This page left intentionally blank)

Ant Anatomy

Label the ant with the following: mandibles, antennae, jointed leg, thorax, abdomen, petiole, head, compound eye.

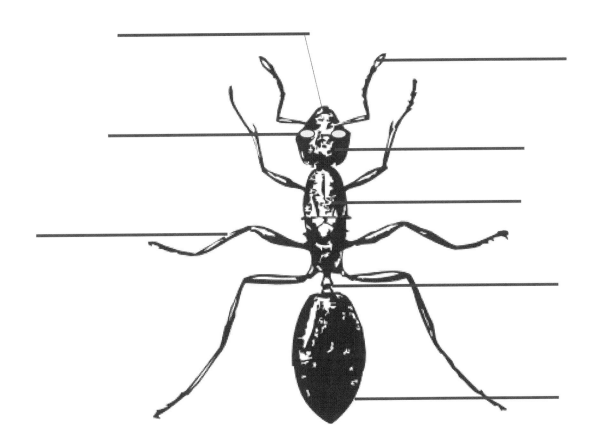

(This page left intentionally blank)

Types of Ants

Cut out each piece and stack them in size order (cover on top, longest piece on bottom). Fill in each piece with facts about the type of ant represented.

Types of ants

Queen ant

(This page left intentionally blank)

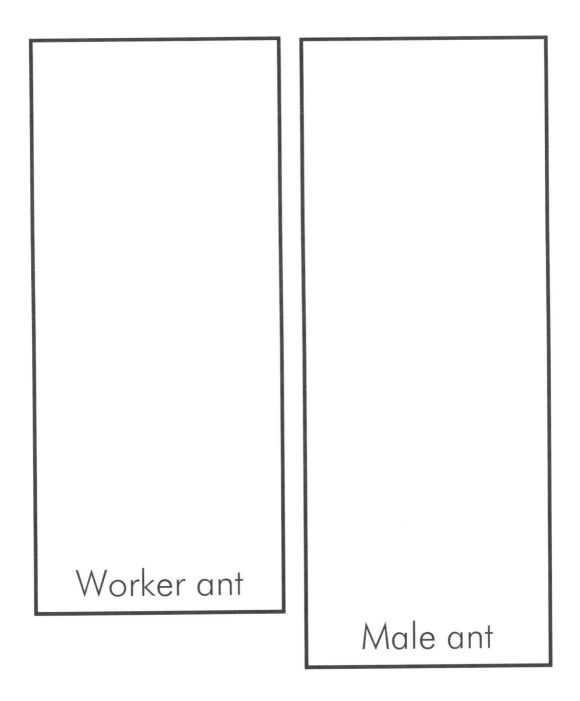

Worker ant

Male ant

(This page left intentionally blank)

Experiment Worksheet

Fill out this worksheet as you work through the experiment.

Question: _____

Hypothesis: _____

_____

Materials: _____

_____

Procedure: _____

_____

_____

_____

_____

Observations/data: _____

_____

_____

_____

_____

Conclusion: _____

_____

_____

(This page left intentionally blank)

(This page left intentionally blank)

Life Span

Cut out the rectangle as one piece and fold on the center line. Cut on the dotted line to the center fold. Inside (opposite the "glue here" side), write the answers.

(glue here)

How long does a worker ant live?

How long does a queen ant live?

(This page left intentionally blank)

Worker Ants

Cut out the clipboard as one piece. Fill in information about the different types of worker ants.

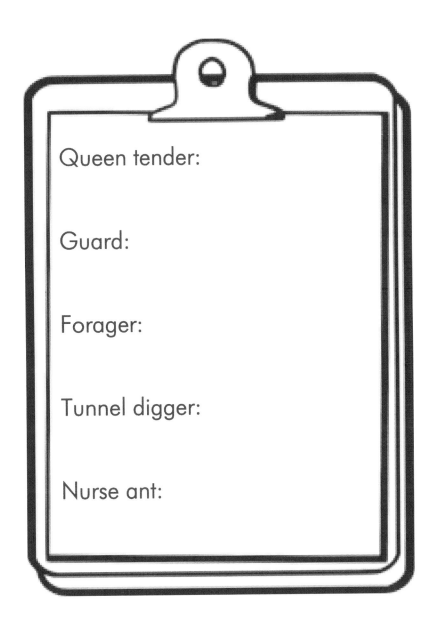

Queen tender:

Guard:

Forager:

Tunnel digger:

Nurse ant:

(This page left intentionally blank)

Ant Communication

Touch

Taste

Smell

Sound

A →

(glue here)

B →

Talk to Me

Cut out the rectangle as one piece. Fold the left side in (on the line at A), and fold the right side in (on the line at B). Cut on the dotted lines so that there are four strips you can open to the fold. On the inside (opposite "glue here"), write facts about how ants use each listed sense to communicate

(This page left intentionally blank)

Ant Life Cycle

Cut around the outside of the first circle, as well as along the dotted lines to cut out the "cut out here" section. Cut around the outside of the second circle. Stack the first circle on the second circle and secure with a brad. Draw each part of the ant life cycle.

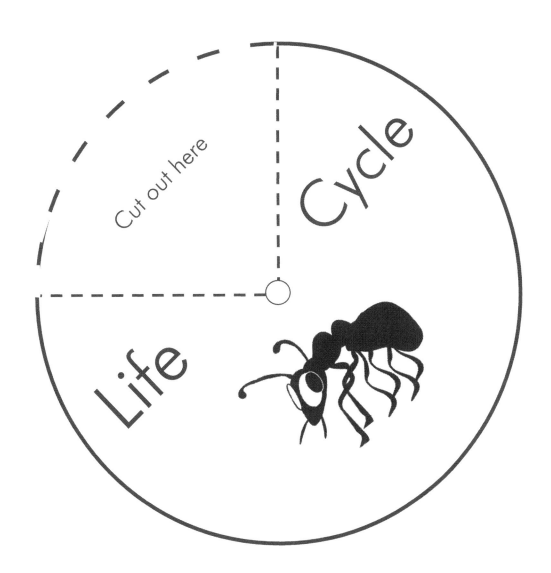

(This page left intentionally blank)

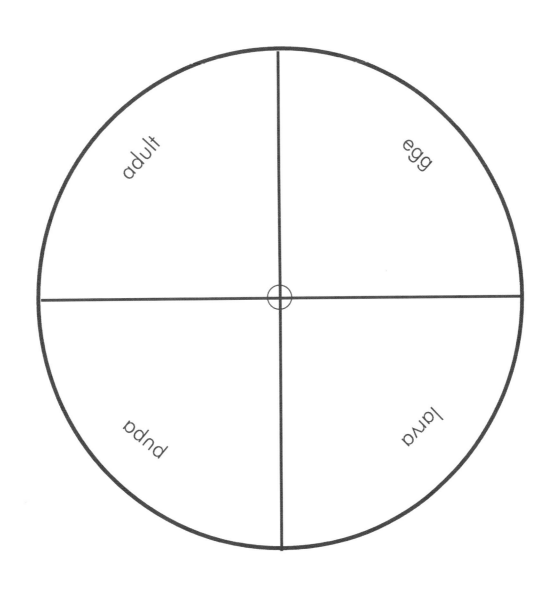

(This page left intentionally blank)

Types of Ants

Research these different types of ants and write interesting facts about them in each minibook.

Leafcutter

(glue here)

Fire

(glue here)

(This page left intentionally blank)

(glue here)

Army

(glue here)

Carpenter

(This page left intentionally blank)

(glue here)

Slave-maker

(glue here)

Harvester

(This page left intentionally blank)

Ant Facts

Use the ant hills to record any ant facts you didn't get to use elsewhere in your lapbook. Stack and staple them and add them to your project.

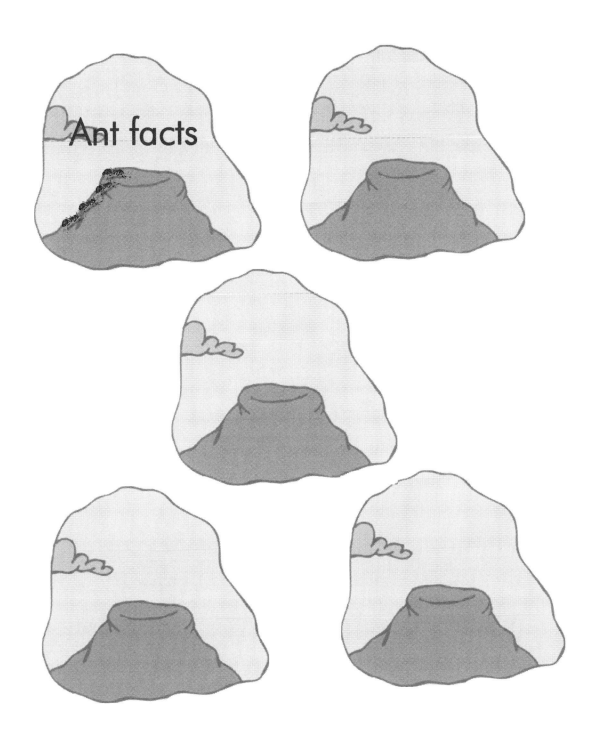

(This page left intentionally blank)

⌐

Ocean Zone Bingo

This page is your bingo board. Instructions for adding the pieces are on the next page. Use coins, small toys, paper clips — any kind of small marker that you can find. Mark off each space as it's called. You can get bingo by getting three in a row in any direction.

Ocean Zone Bingo

Sunlight Zone		
Twilight Zone		
Midnight Zone		

(This page left intentionally blank)

Ocean Zone Bingo

Cut the pieces one row at a time so you don't lose track of where they belong. The top row is the sunlight zone – shuffle them and place them on the top row of your bingo board in random order. The second row is the twilight zone. The third is the midnight zone. There is an extra animal for each zone for variation purposes. The next page is for the "caller."

jellyfish	rays	seaweed	whales
octopus	small crustaceans	viper fish	squid
brittle star	clam	crab	sea cucumber

(This page left intentionally blank)

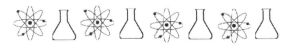

Ocean Zone Bingo

This page is for the "caller." Cut out and mix up all of the pieces. Draw them one at a time from a stack or a bag and have players mark them off their boards as they're called.

jellyfish	rays	seaweed	whales
octopus	small crustaceans	viper fish	squid
brittle star	clam	crab	sea cucumber

(This page left intentionally blank)

Ocean Zones

Use the information about ocean zones to answer the questions.

This zone gets the most sunlight, so plants, such as seaweed, abound. Some common animals of the sunlit zone would be seals, sea turtles, sea lions, manta rays, whales, jellyfish, and sharks.

Sunlit Zone
0-656 feet

A small amount of light reaches the twilight zone, so no plants grow. Octopuses and squid and small crustaceans can be found in this zone.

Twilight Zone
656-3,280 feet

The midnight zone doesn't get any sunlight at all. Some of the animals in this zone don't even have eyes. Anglerfish, snipe eel, and tripod fish can be found in this zone.

Midnight Zone
3,280-13,123 feet

The abyss includes sea creatures that don't have a backbone such as sea spiders. Blind shrimp and hagfish can also be found in the abyss.

Abyss
13,123-19,685 feet

The hadal zone mostly includes frigid parts of the ocean in deep canyons and trenches. Despite the depths and the cold, some life can be found in the hadal zone, including sea cucumbers.

Hadal Zone
19,685-36,197 feet

(This page left intentionally blank)

Ocean Zones

Use the information about ocean zones to answer the questions.

Which ocean zone only gets dim light?

○ Sunlit zone   ○ Twilight Zone   ○ Midnight Zone   ○ Abyss   ○ Hadal Zone

What zone would you be in if you were at 14,000 feet?

○ Sunlit zone   ○ Twilight Zone   ○ Midnight Zone   ○ Abyss   ○ Hadal Zone

Which ocean zone is the deepest?

○ Sunlit zone   ○ Twilight Zone   ○ Midnight Zone   ○ Abyss   ○ Hadal Zone

Which ocean zone gets the most sun light?

○ Sunlit zone   ○ Twilight Zone   ○ Midnight Zone   ○ Abyss   ○ Hadal Zone

Which ocean zone includes plants?

○ Sunlit zone   ○ Twilight Zone   ○ Midnight Zone   ○ Abyss   ○ Hadal Zone

In which ocean zone might you find an anglerfish?

○ Sunlit zone   ○ Twilight Zone   ○ Midnight Zone   ○ Abyss   ○ Hadal Zone

(This page left intentionally blank)

All
About
Sharks

(This page left intentionally blank)

What is a Shark?

Cut out the rectangle as one piece and fold on the dotted line. Inside (opposite the "glue here" side), write information about sharks. Be sure to answer these questions: How many known species of sharks are there? In what sizes to sharks come? What is the most common size? What are sharks' skeletons made of? From where to sharks get their oxygen?

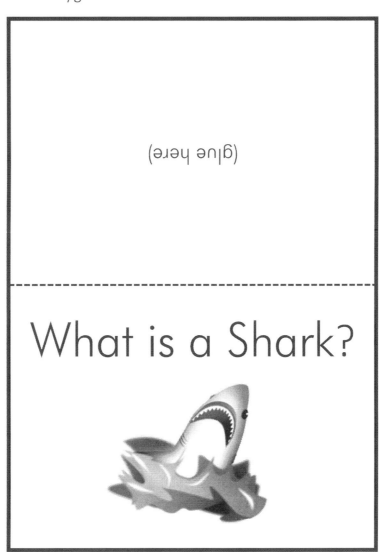

(glue here)

What is a Shark?

(This page left intentionally blank)

Vocabulary

Cut out the beach cards. Define these words as they relate to sharks: cartilage, denticles, gills, predator.

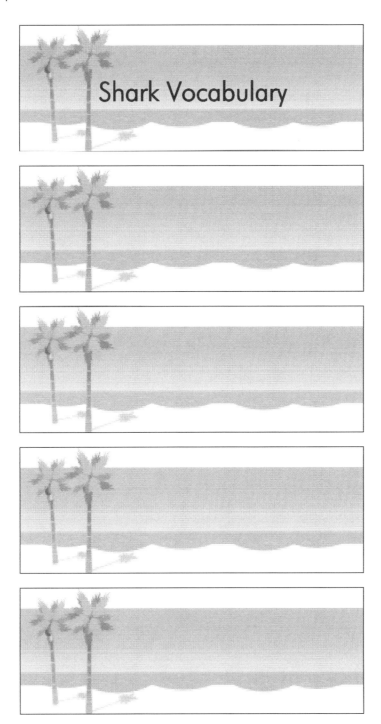

Shark Vocabulary

(This page left intentionally blank)

Shark Sizes

Choose six sharks to research and fill in the graph with their sizes. Cut out the chart and add to your lapbook.

60 feet						
55 feet						
50 feet						
45 feet						
40 feet						
35 feet						
30 feet						
25 feet						
20 feet						
15 feet						
10 feet						
5 feet						
Size ↑						
Type →						

(This page left intentionally blank)

Types of Sharks

Cut out each piece and stack them in size order (cover on top, longest piece on bottom). Write information about each type of shark.

Carpet

Hammerhead

Types of sharks

(This page left intentionally blank)

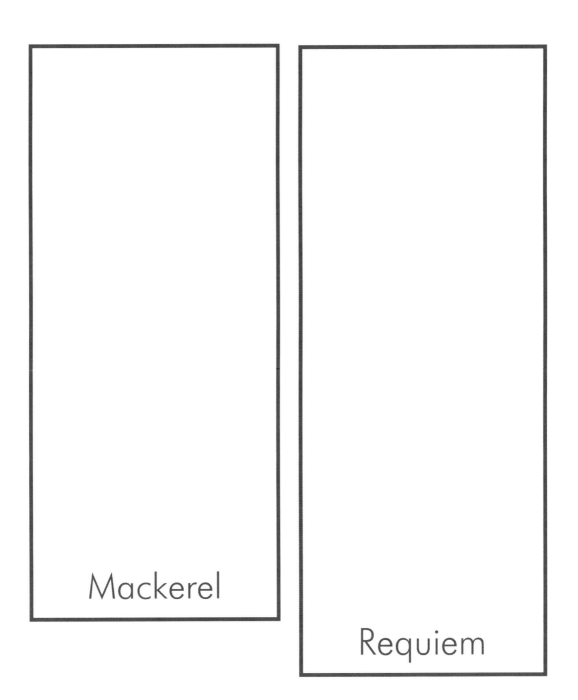

Mackerel

Requiem

(This page left intentionally blank)

Shark Anatomy

Label the shark. Cut out the labeled shark and glue into the middle rectangle of the piece on the left. Cut as one piece and fold the outside squares to cover the shark. Glue the label pieces on top of the folded piece.

Shark
Anatomy

(This page left intentionally blank)

Shark Anatomy

Cut each piece out in full (don't cut off the tab label). Write information on each dotted piece, then cut and glue to a tabbed piece. Stack the pieces so the tabs are in order from left to right with the cover page on top.

Parts of a Shark

Denticles

1

Dorsal Fin

2

(This page left intentionally blank)

Pectoral Fin

3

Caudal Fin

4

Eyes

5

(This page left intentionally blank)

Shark Hunting

Cut out the rectangles and fold on the dotted line. Inside (opposite the "glue here" side), write information about how sharks use their senses to hunt. Here are some questions you can consider: How far away can a shark hear? How far away can a shark smell? What is a lateral line and what does it help a shark detect? What extra sense do sharks have? How do all of these senses help in hunting?

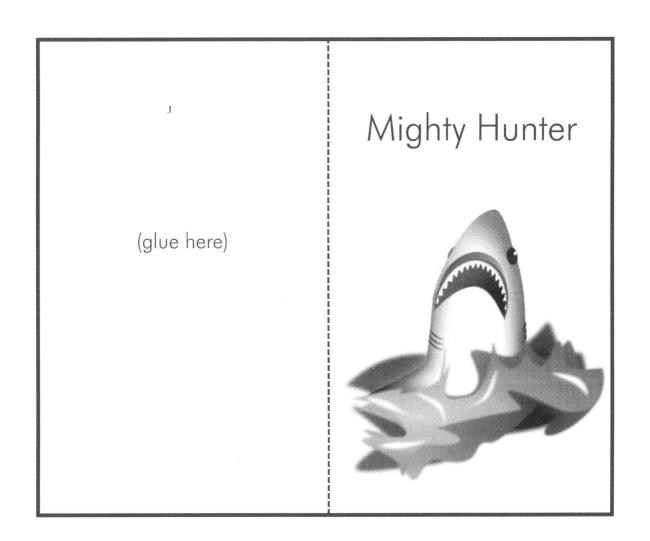

(glue here)

Mighty Hunter

(This page left intentionally blank)

Shark Teeth

Cut out the rectangles and fold on the dotted line. Inside (opposite the "glue here" side), write information about shark teeth. Here are some questions you can answer: how many teeth can a shark have? How many rows of teeth do most sharks have? What happens when a shark loses a tooth?

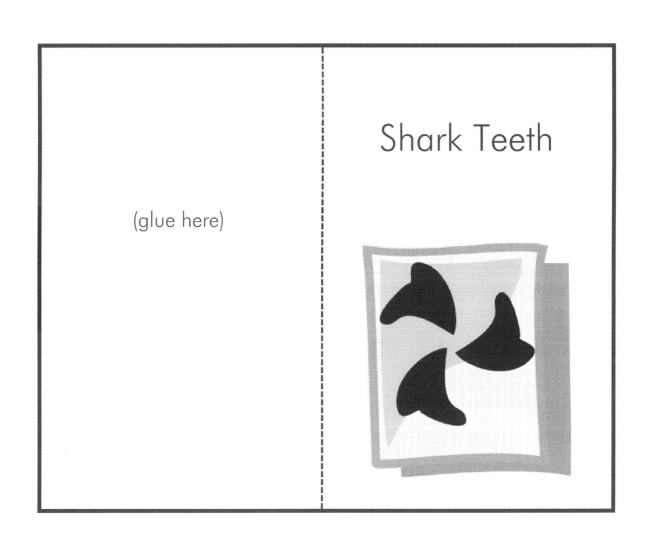

(This page left intentionally blank)

Where Do Sharks Live?

Cut out the hexagons and stack them with the title page on top. Fill in each hexagon with information about where sharks live. Include species names and specifics. Staple and add to your lapbook.

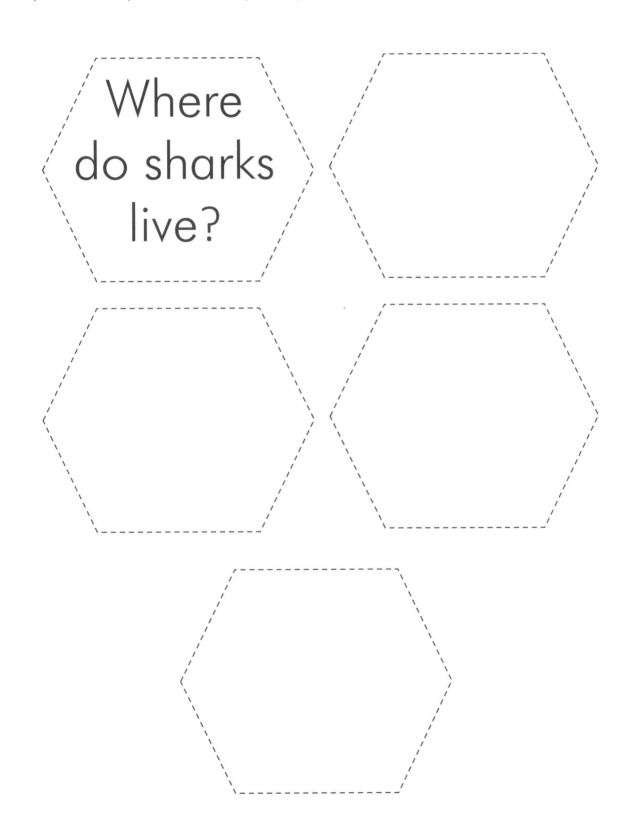

Where do sharks live?

(This page left intentionally blank)

Shark Diet

Cut out the rectangle as one piece and fold on the dotted line. Inside (opposite the "glue here" side), write about what different sharks eat. Consider these questions: What do fast-swimming sharks eat? What do slow-swimming sharks eat? What do filter feeders eat?

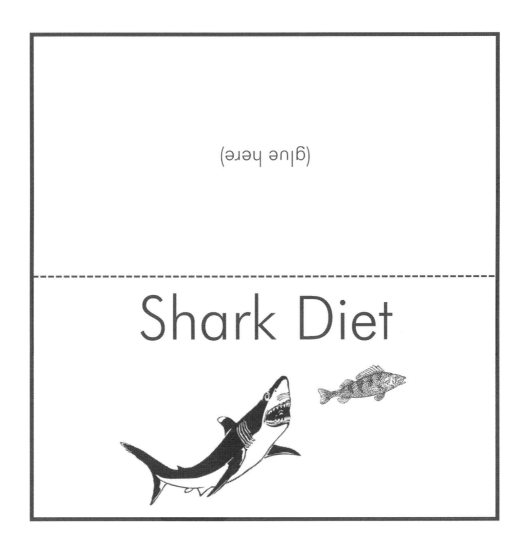

(This page left intentionally blank)

Shark Relatives

Cut out the rectangle as one piece and fold on the dotted line. Inside (opposite the "glue here" side), write about shark relatives – what animals are similar to sharks and why?

Shark Relatives

(glue here)

(This page left intentionally blank)

Baby Shark Do Do Doo...

Cut out the rectangle as one piece and fold on the dotted line. Inside (opposite the "glue here" side), write or paste information about baby sharks. Here are some questions to consider. Where are most shark's eggs hatched? How many baby sharks (pups) can be hatched at once? What can a pup do when it's newly born? What are some dangers for pups?

(glue here)

Baby Sharks

(This page left intentionally blank)

Shark Species

Cut out as one piece. Fold up bottom. Then fold back side tabs and secure to the back flap. You have made a pocket to hold the species cards in your lapbook. Cut out the species cards and write information onto the word card. Store the word cards in the pocket.

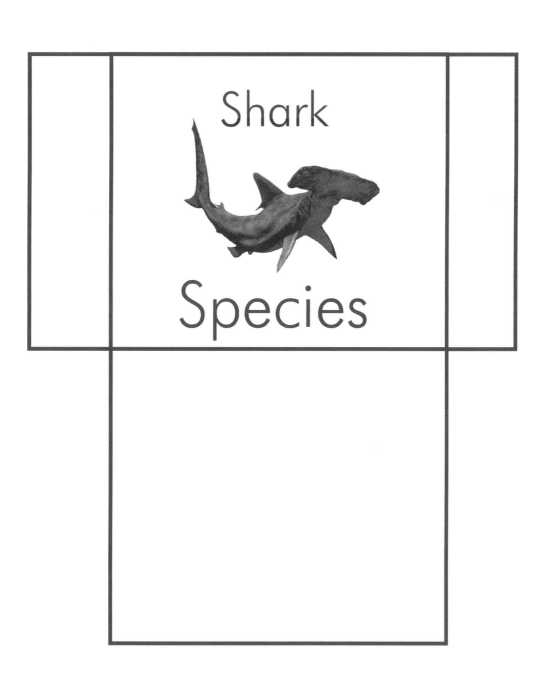

(This page left intentionally blank)

great white

hammerhead

tiger

nurse

(This page left intentionally blank)

whale

lemon

angel

bull

(This page left intentionally blank)

Helping and Hurting

Cut out the rectangle as one piece and fold on the center line. Cut on the dotted line to the center fold. Inside (opposite the "glue here" side), write information about each topic.

(glue here)

How Sharks Help

How Sharks are Hurt

(This page left intentionally blank)

Clam Anatomy

Make a clam. Cut out the whole shape as one piece and fold in half. Cut out a circle from middle, starting at the dot in the middle. You need to fit your pointer finger through it. That is going to be the clam's foot. What do they use their foot for?

(This page left intentionally blank)

Mollusks

Use this page to take notes on the information you read about mollusks. Be sure to use complete sentences.

What are mollusks? _____

_____

_____

_____

What are gastropods? _____

_____

_____

_____

What are cephalopods? _____

_____

_____

_____

What are bivalves? _____

_____

_____

_____

(This page left intentionally blank)

Vocabulary

Fill in the word from the box that best matches the definition given.

crustaceans	nocturnal	flexible	prey
predator	invertebrate	herbivore	camouflage

Able to be bent easily _____

Active at night _____

Concealing oneself by appearing to be
part of one's surroundings _____

An animal that eats other animals _____

Only eats plants _____

Lobsters, crabs, shrimps, and other
segmented arthropods _____

Animal without a backbone _____

An animal that is eaten by other animals _____

(This page left intentionally blank)

Octopus

Use this page to take notes on the information you read. Be sure to use complete sentences.

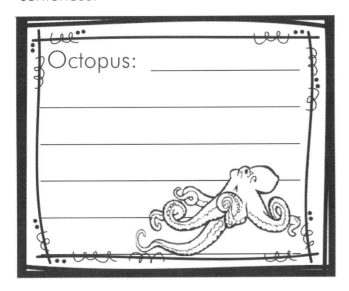

Octopus: _____

Habitat: _____

Diet: _____

Offspring: _____

(This page left intentionally blank)

Octopus

Use this page to take notes on the information you read. Be sure to use complete sentences.

Predators: _____

_____

_____

_____

_____

Color or mark on the map where they are found in the world.

(This page left intentionally blank)

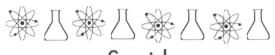

Squid

Use this page to take notes on the information you read. Be sure to use complete sentences.

Squid: _____

Habitat: _____

Diet: _____

Offspring: _____

(This page left intentionally blank)

Squid

Use this page to take notes on the information you read. Be sure to use complete sentences.

Predators: _____

_____

_____

_____

_____

Color or mark on the map where they are found in the world.

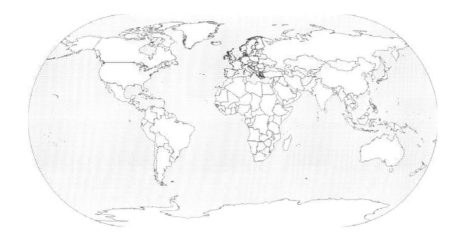

Zoology
Levels 5-8

(This page left intentionally blank)

Snail and Slug

Use this page to take notes on the information you read. Be sure to use complete sentences.

Snail/Slug: _____

Habitat: _____

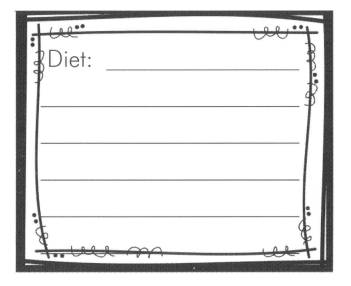

Diet: _____

(This page left intentionally blank)

Snail and Slug

Use this page to take notes on the information you read. Be sure to use complete sentences.

Predators: _____

_____

_____

_____

_____

Color or mark on the map where they are found in the world.

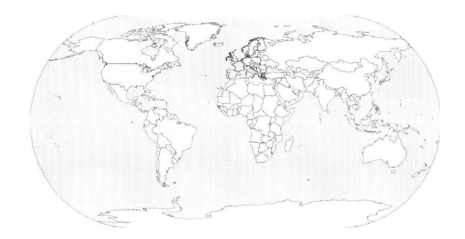

(This page left intentionally blank)

(This page left intentionally blank)

Vocabulary

Use these pages of turtle eggs to record any vocabulary words and definitions that are new to you.

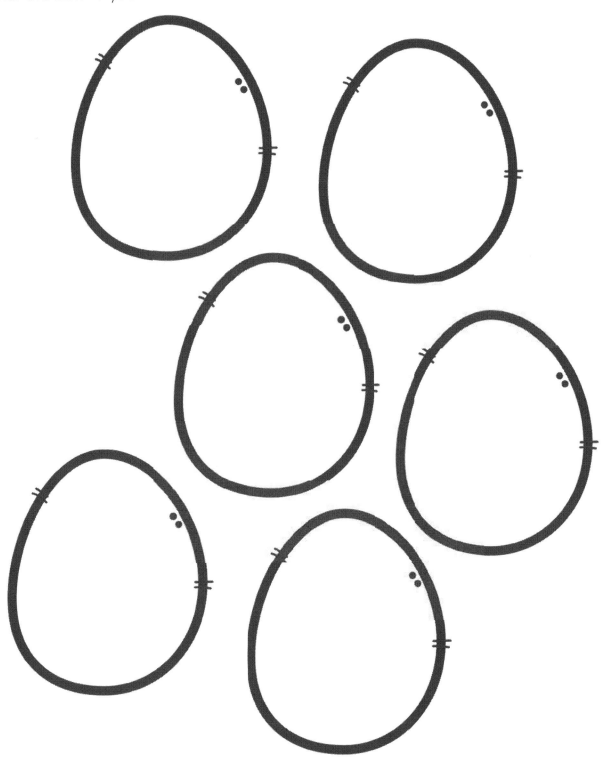

(This page left intentionally blank)

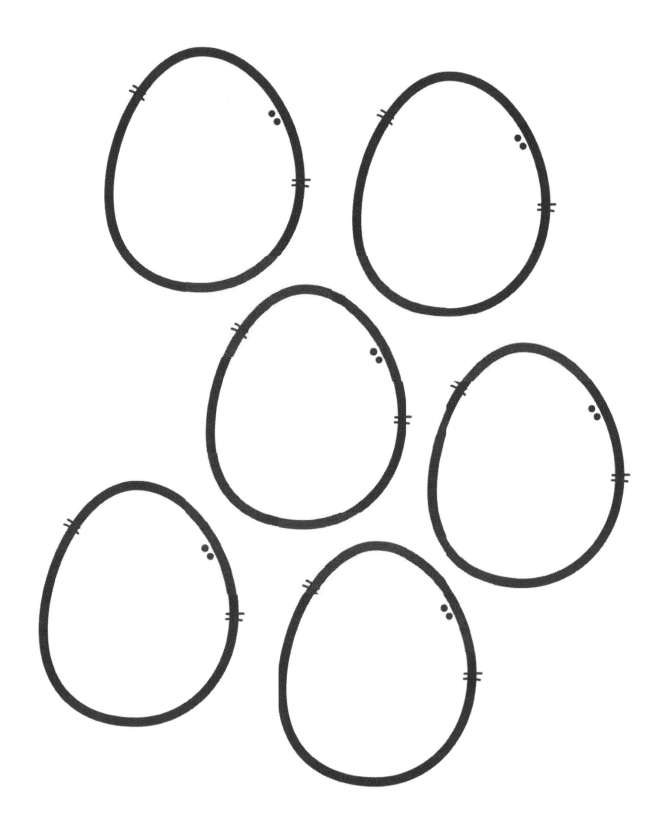

(This page left intentionally blank)

Sea Turtle Facts

Write down some sea turtle facts you found interesting.

(This page left intentionally blank)

Protection

What are some ways turtles are protected from predators?

_____

_____

_____

_____

_____

Types of Reptiles

What are the four types of reptiles?

1. _____

2. _____

3. _____

4. _____

(This page left intentionally blank)

Sea Turtles vs. Other Turtles

What are the similarities and differences between sea turtles and other turtles?

Sea Turtles	Other Turtles
_____	_____
_____	_____
_____	_____
_____	_____
_____	_____
_____	_____
_____	_____

(This page left intentionally blank)

Endangered Species

What does it mean that sea turtles are endangered species?

_____

_____

_____

_____

_____

_____

_____

(This page left intentionally blank)

Sea Turtle Anatomy

Label the parts of the sea turtle.

(This page left intentionally blank)

Sea Turtle Reproduction

What did you learn about sea turtle reproduction?

_____

_____

_____

_____

_____

_____

_____

_____

(This page left intentionally blank)

Sea Turtle Species

Write some facts about each species of sea turtle.

Kemp's Ridley_____

Olive Ridley_____

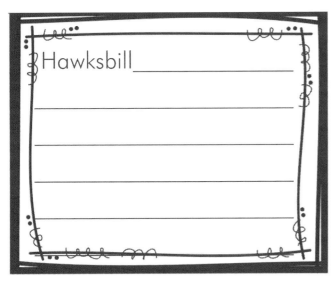

Hawksbill_____

Flatback_____

(This page left intentionally blank)

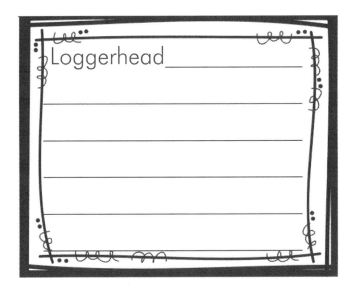

Loggerhead

Green sea turtle

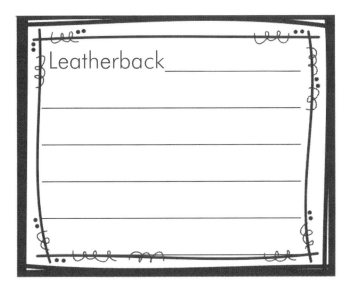

Leatherback

(This page left intentionally blank)

Compare and Contrast

Compare and contrast feedlots and pastures.

Pastures   Feedlots

_____   _____

_____   _____

_____   _____

_____   _____

_____   _____

_____   _____

_____   _____

_____   _____

_____   _____

_____   _____

_____   _____

(This page left intentionally blank)

Cow Classification

Fill in the levels of cow classification.

Kingdom: _____

Phylum: _____

Class: _____

Order: _____

Suborder: _____

Family: _____

Genus: _____

Species: _____

(This page left intentionally blank)

Cow Anatomy

Write some facts about each part of a cow's anatomy.

Appearance: _____

_____

_____

_____

_____

Udders: _____

_____

_____

_____

_____

_____

_____

Teeth_____

_____

_____

_____

Horns_____

_____

_____

_____

_____

_____

_____

(This page left intentionally blank)

Feet_____

Digestive System____

(This page left intentionally blank)

Cattle History

Fill in the answers as you read about cattle history.

Cattle originated here:

_____
_____
_____
_____

Cattle were brought to America in 1493 by:

_____
_____

More cattle were brought in 1600 by:

_____

The first cattle in the United States were

_____

brought from

_____

(This page left intentionally blank)

All
About
Marsupials

(This page left intentionally blank)

Herbivore or Carnivore

Cut out the rectangle as one piece and fold on the center line. Cut on the dotted line to the center fold. Inside (opposite the "glue here" side), sort the marsupials into the proper categories.

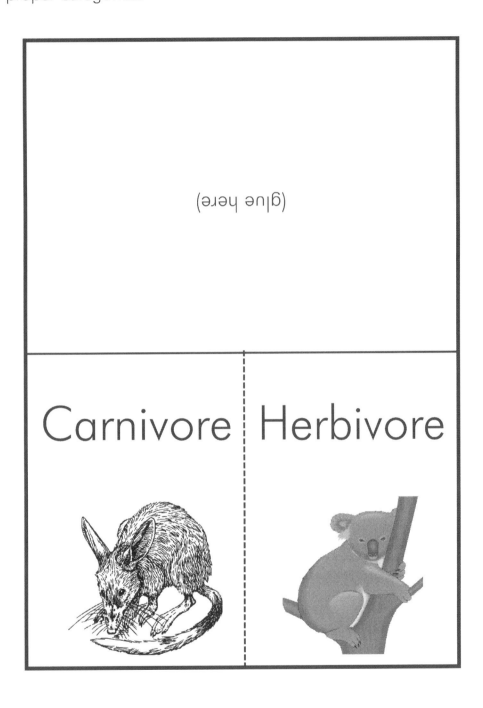

Pouches

Cut the piece out in full and fold on the dotted line. Write what you learned about marsupial pouches inside.

Why the
Pouch?

(This page left intentionally blank)

Kangaroos

Cut each piece out in full and fold on the dotted line. Write what you learned about kangaroo diets and information about joeys.

Kangaroo
Diet

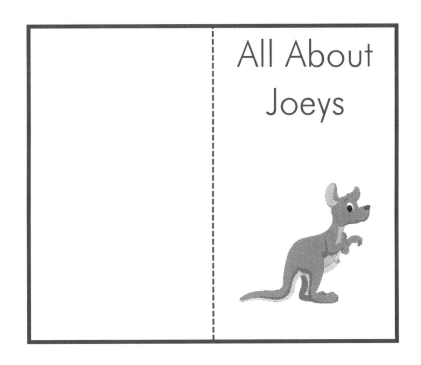

All About
Joeys

(This page left intentionally blank)

Kangaroos

Cut out the rectangles and fold on the dotted line. Inside (opposite the "glue here" side), write about kangaroo tails and how far they can jump, then about kangaroo behavior.

(glue here)

Kangaroo
Tails

(glue here)

Kangaroo
Behavior

(This page left intentionally blank)

Kangaroo Facts

Cut out the hexagons and stack them with the title page on top. Fill in any other facts about kangaroos you'd like to include in your lapbook.

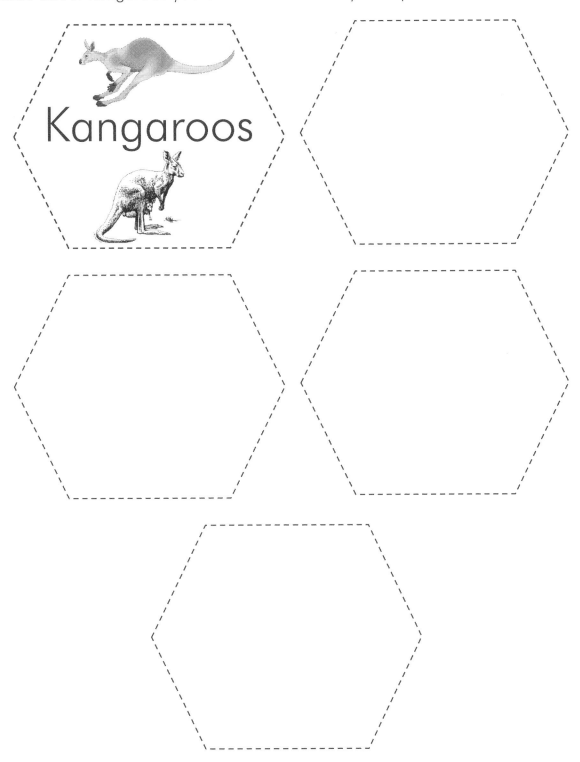

Kangaroos

(This page left intentionally blank)

Koalas

Cut out each piece and stack them in size order (cover on top, longest piece on bottom). Write information about each category as it pertains to koalas.

Habitat

Diet

Koalas

(This page left intentionally blank)

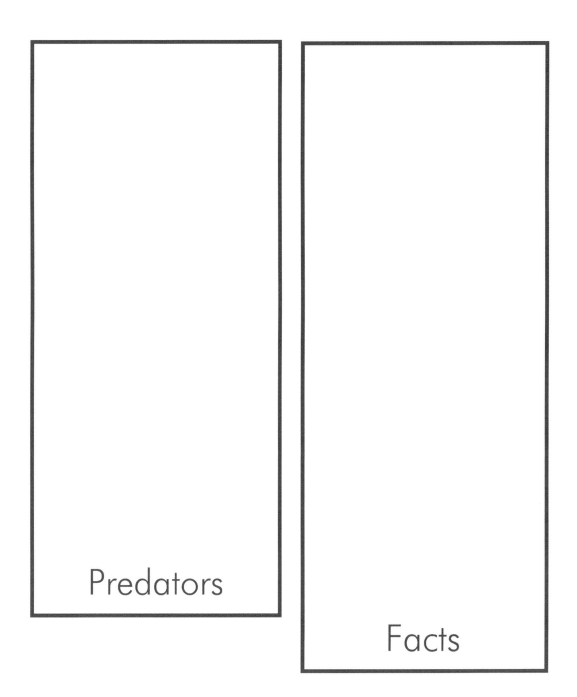

Predators

Facts

(This page left intentionally blank)

Opossum Anatomy

Cut each piece out in full (don't cut off the tab label). Write information on each piece. Stack the pieces in this order top to bottom: Opossum Anatomy, paws, tail, ears.

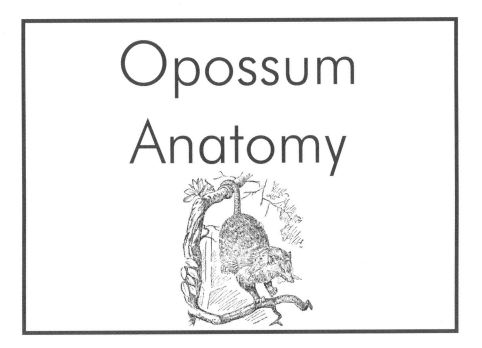

paws

(This page left intentionally blank)

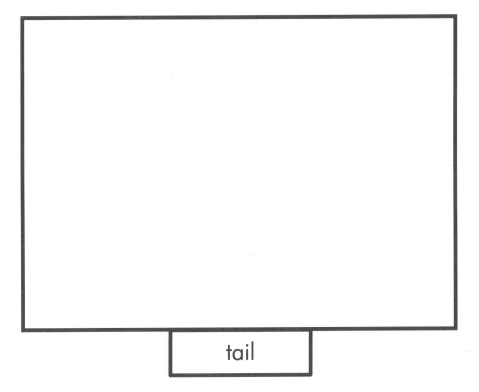

tail

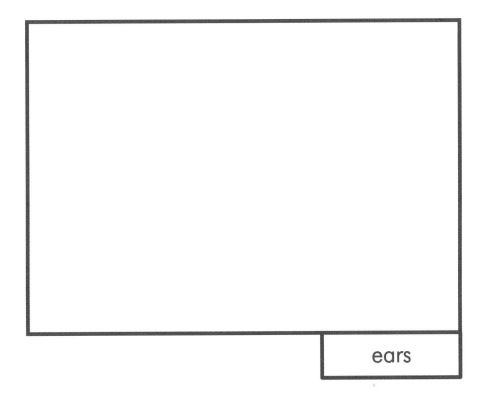

ears

(This page left intentionally blank)

Opossum Facts

Cut the big rectangle as one piece and fold the outside squares in over top of the rectangle. Glue the label pieces on top of the folded piece. Write interesting facts about opossums inside. Include in your facts what it means to "play possum."

(This page left intentionally blank)

Tasmanian Devil

Cut out the rectangle as one piece and fold on the dotted line. Inside (opposite the "glue here" side), write facts about Tasmanian devils. Be sure to include what happens when they get mad.

(glue here)

Tasmanian Devils

(This page left intentionally blank)

Other Marsupials

Cut each piece out in full (don't cut off the tab label). Write information on each piece. Stack the pieces in this order top to bottom: Other Marsupials, wombat, numbat, bandicoot, wallaby.

Other Marsupials

wombat

(This page left intentionally blank)

numbat

bandicoot

(This page left intentionally blank)

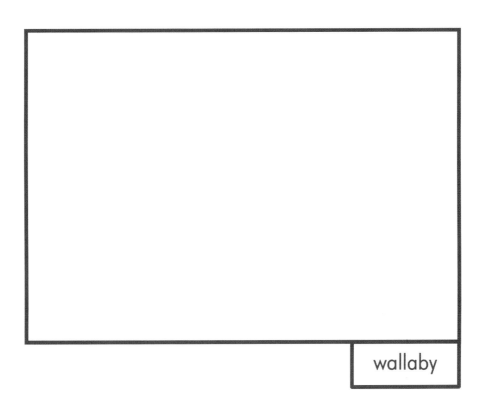

wallaby

(This page left intentionally blank)

Lapbook Pieces

Use the cards for vocabulary, sorting, matching, or other information.

(This page left intentionally blank)

Lapbook Pieces

Cut out as one piece. Fold up bottom. Then fold back side tabs and secure to the back flap. You have made a pocket to hold the cards from the previous page.

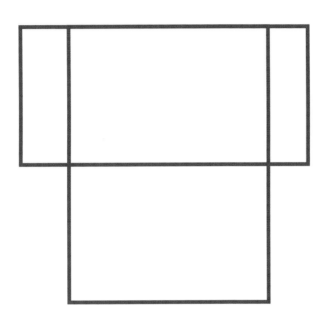

(This page left intentionally blank)

Lapbook Pieces

Cut out each piece as one and fold them in half. Write information inside. Put titles on each piece.

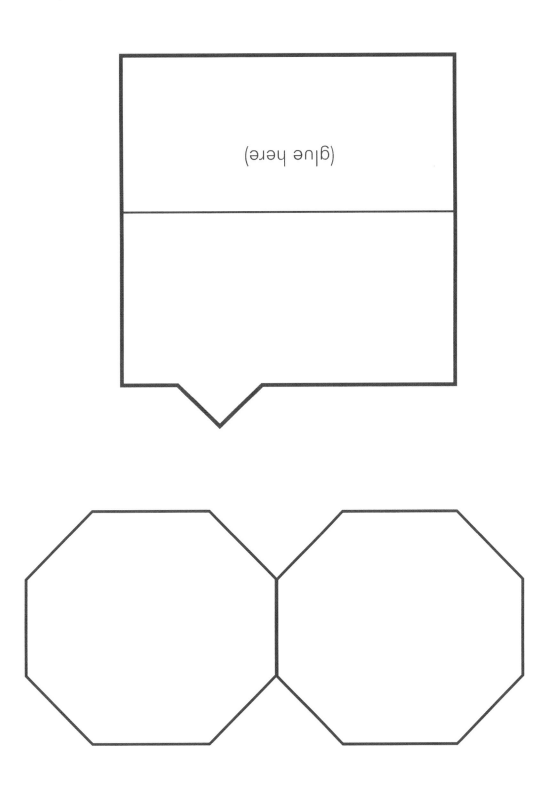

(glue here)

(This page left intentionally blank)

Lapbook pieces

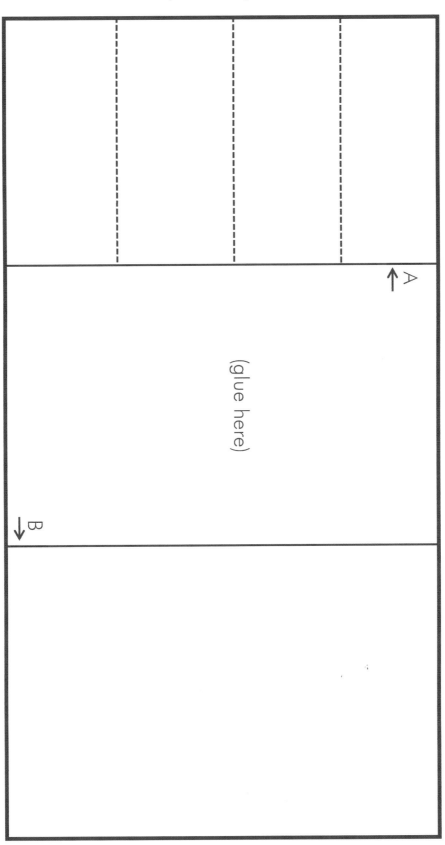

A

B

(glue here)

Cut out the rectangle as one piece. Fold the left side in (on the line at **A**), and fold the right side in (on the line at **B**). Cut on the dotted lines so you have four strips you can label and open to the fold. On the inside (opposite "glue here"), write your information. On the right panel, create a title and add artwork if you'd like.

(This page left intentionally blank)

Lapbook pieces

Cut out the rectangle as one piece and fold on the center line. Cut on the dotted line to the center fold. Label the two flaps. Inside (opposite the "glue here" side), write your information.

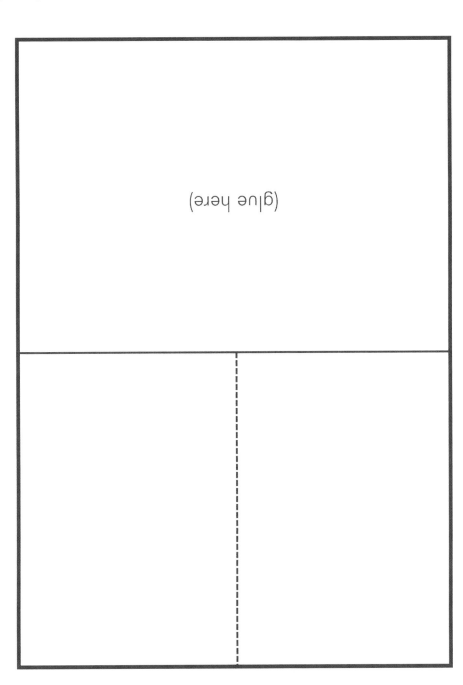

(This page left intentionally blank)

Lapbook pieces

Cut out the rectangles and fold on the dotted line. Label the right side and add artwork if you'd like. Inside (opposite the "glue here" side), write your information.

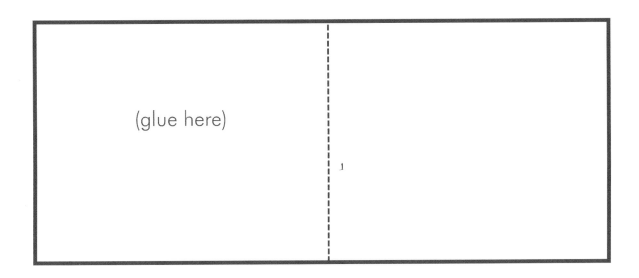

(glue here)

(glue here)

(This page left intentionally blank)

(glue here)

(glue here)

(This page left intentionally blank)

Lapbook Pieces

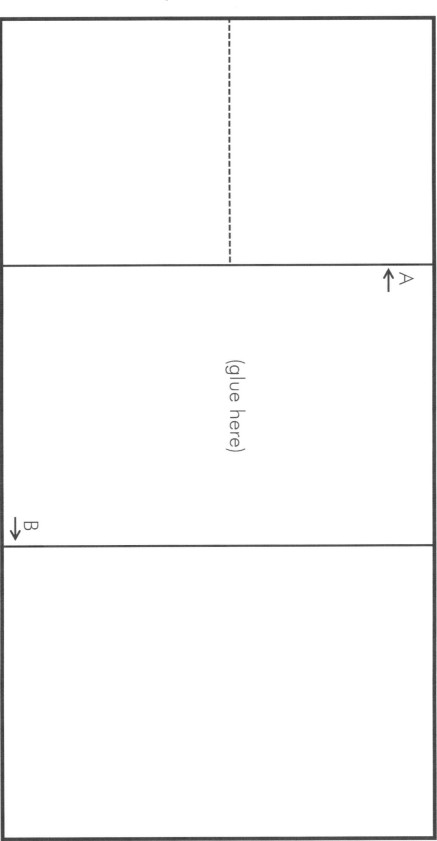

Cut out the rectangle as one piece. Fold the left side in (on the line at **A**), and fold the right side in (on the line at **B**). Cut on the dotted line so that there are two strips you can open to the fold. This piece is good for comparing and contrasting or talking about two characteristics of an animal. Use the right panel to title the piece and include artwork if you want to.

(This page left intentionally blank)

Lapbook Pieces

Cut out the hexagons. Add a title and/or artwork to one piece and information to the other pieces. Stack them and staple on the side to make a book.

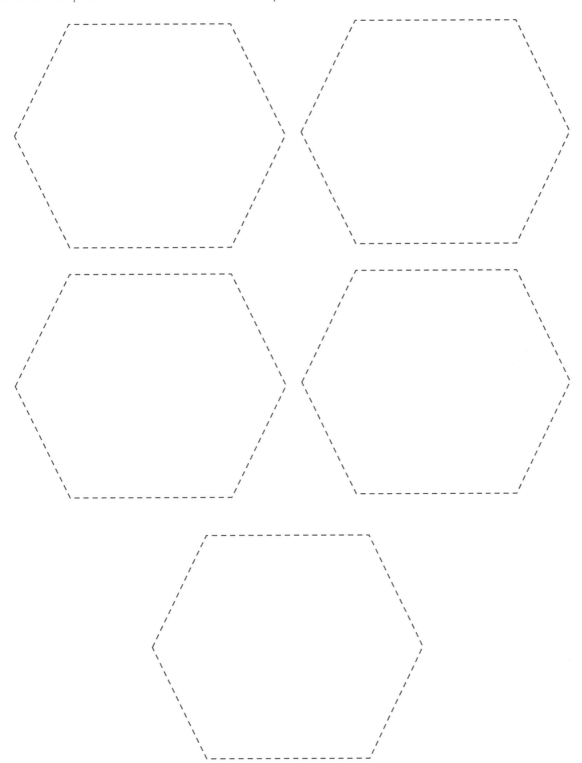

(This page left intentionally blank)

Lapbook pieces

Cut out the rectangle as one piece and fold on the dotted line. Give the piece a title and/or artwork. Inside (opposite the "glue here" side), write your information.

(glue here)

(This page left intentionally blank)

(glue here)

(This page left intentionally blank)

Lapbook Pieces

Cut out as one piece. Fold up bottom. Then fold back side tabs and secure to the back flap. Label the pocket. You have made a pocket to hold the verse cards in your lapbook. Cut out the cards. Fill in information and store them in the pocket.

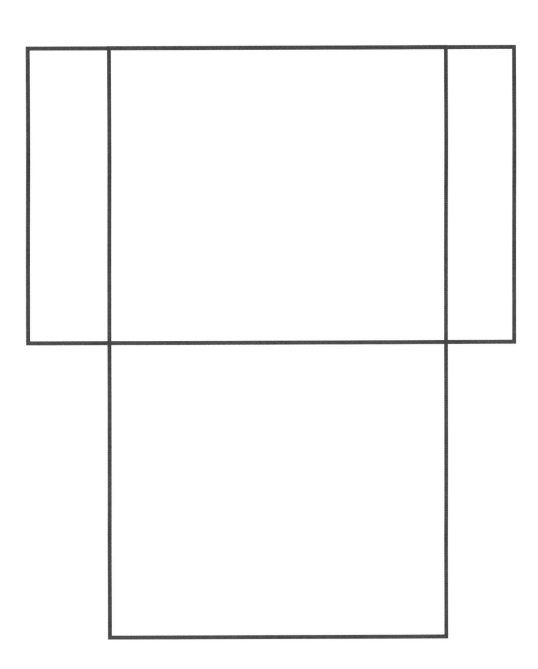

(This page left intentionally blank)

(This page left intentionally blank)

Lapbook pieces

Cut each piece out in full (don't cut off the tab label). The piece without the tab is the cover – add a title and/or artwork. Be sure to label each tab and stack them in order: cover, left tab, center tab, right tab.

(This page left intentionally blank)

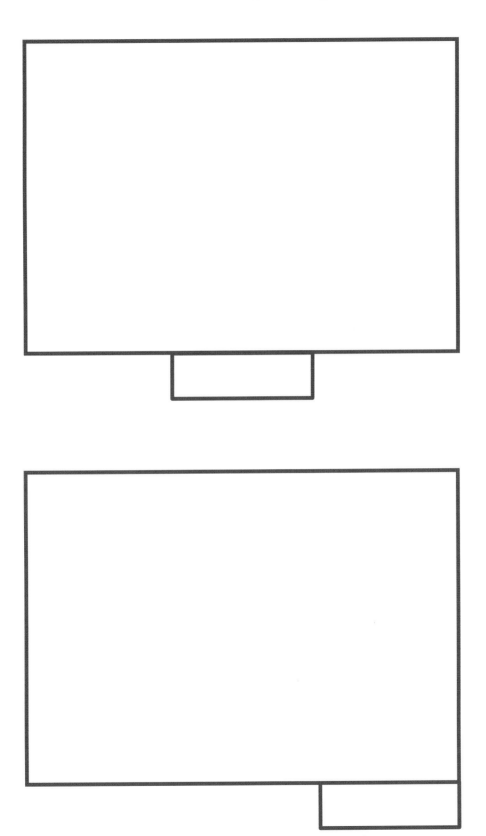

(This page left intentionally blank)

Lapbook Pieces

Cut out each piece and stack them in size order (shortest piece on top, longest piece on bottom). Label the bottom of each piece and fill in information.

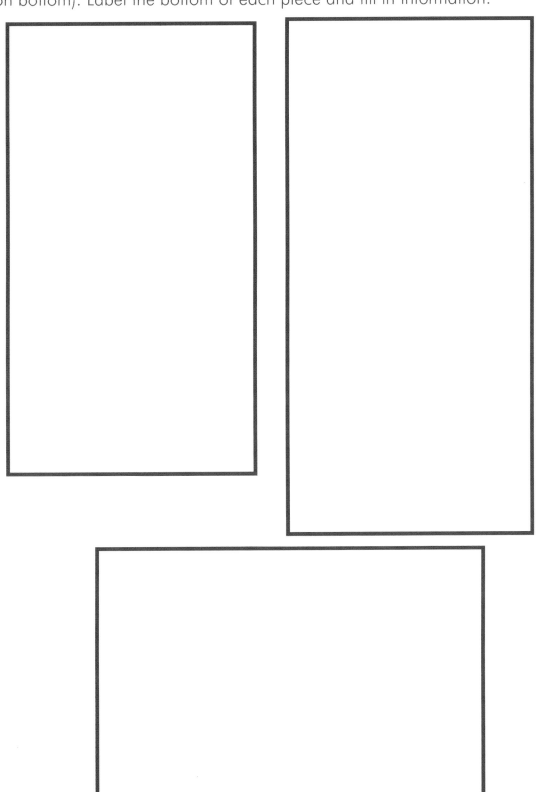

(This page left intentionally blank)

(This page left intentionally blank)

Lapbook Pieces

Cut each piece out in full and fold each piece on the dotted line. Write a title on the big book. Give each small book a topic and put facts inside. Glue the three small pieces side by side inside of the large piece.

(glue here)

(This page left intentionally blank)

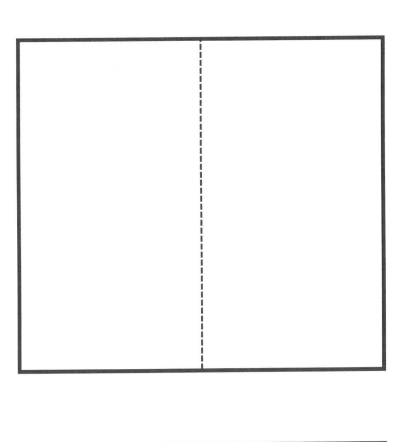

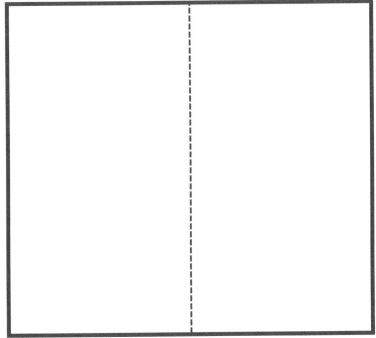

(This page left intentionally blank)

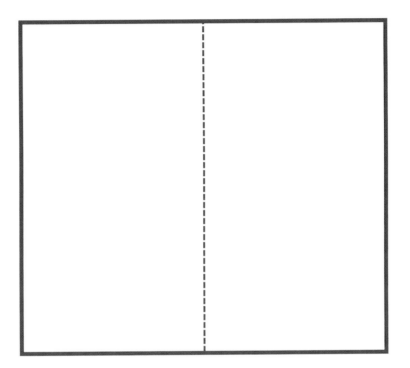

」

(This page left intentionally blank)

(This page left intentionally blank)

Lapbook pieces

Cut around the outside of the first circle, as well as along the dotted lines to cut out the "cut out here" section. Put a title and/or artwork on this circle. Cut around the outside of the second circle. Fill each wedge of the circle with a fact (you can add more artwork if you have too many wedges). Stack the first circle on the second circle and secure with a brad.

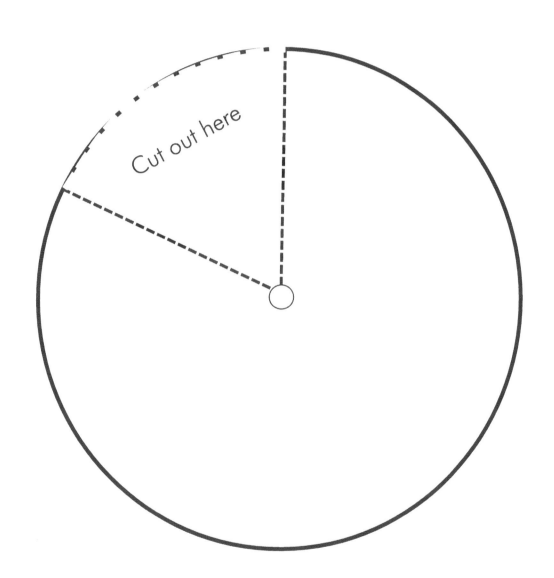

Cut out here

(This page left intentionally blank)

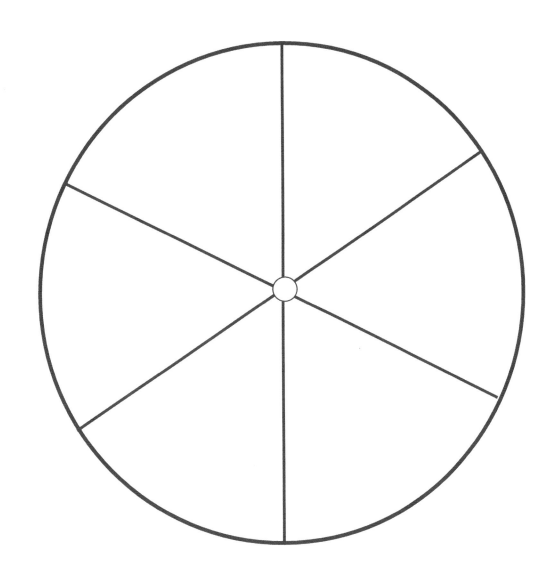

(This page left intentionally blank)

Lapbook Pieces

Cut out the map and the key. Color in the map to show where in the world you can find your animal. Be sure to mark the key.

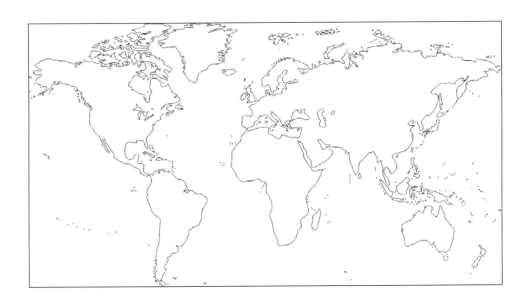

Key

(This page left intentionally blank)

Lapbook Pieces

Cut out the rectangles and fold on the dotted line. Inside (opposite the "glue here" side), write your information. Be sure to add a title and artwork if you desire.

(glue here)

(glue here)

Zoology
Levels 5-8

(This page left intentionally blank)

Lapbook Pieces

Cut as one piece and fold the outside squares to cover the middle. Label the piece and add artwork if you'd like.

(This page left intentionally blank)

Experiment Worksheet

Fill out this worksheet as you work through the experiment.

Question: _____

Hypothesis: _____

_____

Materials: _____

_____

Procedure: _____

_____

_____

_____

_____

Observations/data: _____

_____

_____

_____

_____

Conclusion: _____

_____

_____

(This page left intentionally blank)

Research Notes

Use these pages to make notes on your topic.

Topic:_____

Resource 1:_____

Info:_____   Info:_____

Info:_____   Info:_____

Info:_____   Info:_____

Resource 2:_____

Info:_____   Info:_____

Info:_____   Info:_____

Info:_____   Info:_____

Resource 3:_____

Info:_____   Info:_____

Info:_____   Info:_____

Info:_____   Info:_____

Resource 4:_____

Info:_____   Info:_____

Info:_____   Info:_____

Info:_____   Info:_____

(This page left intentionally blank)

Resource 5:_____

Info:_____   Info:_____

Info:_____   Info:_____

Info:_____   Info:_____

Resource 6:_____

Info:_____   Info:_____

Info:_____   Info:_____

Info:_____   Info:_____

Resource 7:_____

Info:_____   Info:_____

Info:_____   Info:_____

Info:_____   Info:_____

Resource 8:_____

Info:_____   Info:_____

Info:_____   Info:_____

Info:_____   Info:_____

Resource 9:_____

Info:_____   Info:_____

Info:_____   Info:_____

Info:_____   Info:_____

(This page left intentionally blank)

Science Report Checklist

Use this checklist to help you as you finish up your science project. Aim for a checkmark in each box.

Research
☐ Facts
☐ Sources
☐ Bibliography

Project
☐ 3D
☐ Neat
☐ Teaches all about your topic; shows off all you learned
☐ Self-explanatory: someone could look at it and understand what it's all about without you explaining it to them
☐ Bibliography displayed with project

Experiment
☐ Demonstrates your topic
☐ Neatly written up with all parts of the experiment worksheet
☐ Able to be done over and over with the same results

Demonstration
☐ Clearly state what your project is about
☐ Tell about what they will learn from your project
☐ Explain how the experiment relates to your topic
☐ Demonstrate the experiment
☐ State your conclusion
☐ Ask if anyone has questions

Made in the USA
Columbia, SC
24 September 2024